Fireflies

Fireflies

MAYA KHANDELWAL

PARTRIDGE

To order additional copies of this book, contact
Partridge India
000 800 10062 62
orders.india@partridgepublishing.com

www.partridgepublishing.com/india

Foreword

The diary is every teenager's friend and confidante, and here we find a bunch of teenagers, pouring out their aches and anguish, shreds of loneliness, slivers of hope, bursts of anger and existential angst in their dairies.

The diaries are the shoulders they cry on, be it grumbling about their friends - turned foes, confiding about their dependence on drugs, or talking about pangs of guilt, bouts of jealousies- it is here in their diaries that we can see them wringing their hands, gritting their teeth, and yearning to be whole, once again.

What I found absolutely endearing about the book is the teenage lingo that the author uses.

The linguistic purists might crinkle their noses at this, but that is the way teenagers speak, don't they?

It is this lingo that brings a smile to the readers' lips, giving a touch of authenticity to the book.

This intriguing book, gives us a peep into teenagers' psyche, their trials and tribulations, the dreams pulsating in their hearts, the nightmares plaguing them, the agony and the ecstasy, remorse and regret, which follow them at every step.

The teenage world is full of peer pressure, bouts of depression, suicidal moods, crushes, breakups, fear of ragging and other vulnerabilities and the book takes everything into account.

While reading the book, I found myself crying, laughing, sighing and sobbing with the teenagers, oscillating between triumph and disaster, and finally emerging an enriched person.

I loved this book, as much as I loved the author's first book, A Beautiful Mistake.

This is a book not only for every teenager, but also for every teenager's parents.

Dr Santosh Bakaya

*Writer of critically acclaimed **BALLAD OF BAPU** and **Where are the Lilacs?***

Santosh has received the International Reuel Award for writing and literature 2014, for her poem OH HARK!

Reviews

A Beautiful Mistake

Maya's Debut Novel

Magicality of Love

What happens when a girl from a typical Punjabi, middle class family, strikes a friendship with a boy from a different caste? It's a random phone call that sets things rolling; a wrong number becomes the right number, meandering through slip-ups, mishaps, and pangs of separation. Packed with fun, frolic, spunk, joy and excitement, this is the touching story of a girl who does not want to go through life as a submissive and flimsy girl, reluctant to be a mere doll, living in a doll's house, but a girl with a will of her own. Peopled with finely delineated characters you will find in every Indian home, complete with their warts, fears, and misgivings, it is a delightful read. As you eavesdrop on the sweet- nothings of the phone friends, a smile erupts on your lips. Haven't you heard it all before, been part of it somewhere down the line?

The book leaves one drenched in the colours of love that the writer splashes, so sensitively. Small apprehensions, smaller doubts gaining gigantic magnitude, one can see it all, feel it all, it is so palpable. Real flesh and blood characters move around you, pulling you in their midst.

Garnished liberally with dollops of humour, yearnings, nostalgia, a girl's fears and insecurities, qualms of a young middle class girl on the threshold of marriage and pangs of guilt, Maya Khandelwal's pen tackles everything effortlessly.

A book so riveting, that it can be finished in one sitting, and leave you craving for more. The surprise ending leaves you with a never ending Cheshire grin. A book you need to grab immediately, if you believe in the magicality of love.

And yes, the cover of the book by Partridge is as charming as the book itself.

Dr Santosh Bakaya

*****

Soft Romance

Maya Khandelwal's debut novel, A Beautiful Mistake is all reality and no Maya (illusion). It revives the old world charm of soft romance and softer conflicts of life faced by the lovers. The story revolves around a strangely begun love affair and how it culminates into marriage. The love birds belong to different castes and the age old parental tyranny plays the villain in the novel. Maya has an eye for the finer details of her surroundings. Everything she describes, she describes with authenticity and creates an ambience one can feel and see. She has got that magical language to take the reader to a journey inside and outside her characters. While reading the novel I too went down memory lane and reached the romantic land of my youth. In today's jet age Maya's soft flowing sentences and emotional expressions may soothe the readers. In fact, her style becomes her carrier of emotions and deeper feelings. Her use of shorter sentences for deep emotions and long flowing sentences for creating the right atmosphere for the outburst of such emotions is a quality of her own. Instead of the racy style used by today's pop writers she has chosen a mild and wavy style of writing and no doubt, it is commendablein the sense that she has decided to flow against the wind of modernity.

I hope the graph of her writing career will rise and rise with every new book she writes and she does not feel satisfied by writing popcorn novels. She must focus on the harder conflicts of life faced by the common people around her to prove herself as a conscientious author.

NEELABH PANDIT
Head of English Department
Govt. Commerce College
Alwar Rajasthan

*****

A Love Story with Real Mundane Bumps and Divine Solutions

An adolescent girl falls in love with a boy per chance. The love story has been successfully interwoven with the mundane problems and divine solutions in the life of two innocent adults. It entails the problems that come in the way of the couple and presents a realistic view of the situations that surmount in the marital life. Some times in life, we wonder the couples who get married with the bond of love... per their choice... in the presence of Cupid..., what comes between them...this book describes...it in its own beautiful way and the divine solutions are also there.... to read it has been a nice experience. A love story with the in depth details of psyche of a girl. As a feminine writer, she has been very successful in depicting the pleasures and sorrows as felt by the fair gender at its heart; such description of feminine psyche is rare and at some instances in the book is unforgettable.

Deo Malik
AGM S.B.B.J.
Alwar

*****

Delightful & Gripping!

After having gone through the novel- a common story coupled with, in-depth description of Nature and powerful emotions recollected in tranquillity by the lead character, I take pleasure to state that future has lot of admiration in store for her as a writer. What one has achieved in life through natural abilities, not relying on luck, family background or social ambience, shall happen to be a deciding factor for making most of life one has got. It is only through reciprocal exchange of compassion that life never gets mundane or boring. The interesting tale of Mansi, the epitome of a compassionate heart, who could manage to survive against inertia and overwhelming odds in her life, leaves a trail to follow and at best deserves a hats-off as her maiden effort. Happy endings are made all the more poignant by the memory of unhappy beginnings.

With all good wishes
Advocate Krishna Kumar,
Alwar

*****

Mesmerising!

That moment when something is troubling you to the core of your heart but in a mesmerising way! The feeling when you get pushed into someone's dreams almost unknowingly!

Would you call it a mistake? Of course not! It will be more of a beautiful mistake.

Muskaan Jain
Student

*****

A Captivating Love Call

The novel urges you to see life in an entire different way. Relationships can make or mar your life. Let them be nourished by little sacrifices and mutual trust.

Mansi, the central character listens to her heart both when she allows Aditya to steal her heart and when she has to prioritise between love and ambition. That's how even her mistakes become favourite.

Kashish Khandelwal
Scholar

*****

A Tender Love Story

Maya Khandelwal's lyrical love stories `Beautiful Mistake' is a story of two people from two different backgrounds, deeply in love with each other, discovering altogether a new world. It's a real story of a young woman sharing her inner and outer struggles not only for love but for the choice she made, all by herself. The choices, decisions taken by a female are not readily accepted in our society. The beauty of this tender love story lies in the fact that how a young lady loves her counterpart without losing her own self and her values. The story is gripping and sharply written but is racy enough to give its reader the experience of life time and take them to another world. It is hard to believe that it's penned by a first timer.

Dr.Shafali Barathonia

Associate professor of Political Science

G.D.Govt.Girls College, Alwar (Raj)

Writer of two books: 'Mahatma Gandhi aur Vishva' and 'Bhartiya Rajnay' (Indian diplomacy) Author of many research articles in various national and International journals.

*****

A Motivational Book!

A book that answers millions of couples questions in the turbulent urban life! It has beautifully carved the characters, their emotions and the depth of every relation. The story is woven around the internal conflict of the girl who on one side tries to win the battle of love and on the other side, has lots of sacrifices to make. Brimming with romance, ego, suspense... it can surely win over a reader's heart and mind! The impact of this book on me has been really boosting and positive. Lots of aspects, hidden in small incidents of your quotidian which we merely approve. Let's explore our inner souls and help ourselves to overcome the barriers of life. Why not begin with A Beautiful Mistake!! :)

Mehak Bhargava
Sophomore'19
Computer Engineering
Gonzaga University

*****

A Love Filled Freshness!

The innocence of budding young heart and slow transition to the unknown path of love is beautifully worded till the end of the story. The strength of love to face anything and everything is depicted in all purity while narrating incidences. A love filled freshness!!!

Rajshree Kaul
Spiritual Psychic Healer, Counsellor and Guide
Master Teacher of Healing Modalities

*****

Author's Note

Birthing a book is a beautiful journey inside out. It's an urge to recede into the fictional world when you have had your fleeting fill of reading the world around. AND it needs to be recorded at once. While making this particular journey, I have wandered into realms all new, imagined myself into the skin of these lovely souls called teenagers. I have dreamt their dreams, felt their vulnerabilities, wept their tears, hummed their songs and also laughed their laughter.

I have learnt the unique slang terms and catch phrases so much so that my PC has given up correcting those!

I'm of the generation when there were no mobile phones and our parents were sweetly ignorant of where we were. As children we did make mistakes, got punished but we never sulked or had any psychological problems about feeling unloved or ignored. Our parents sought no help from psychotherapists to assess as to what bothered us. We did fail in exams. We flunked. We loved. We failed in love but...somehow we managed to survive.

I have observed how teenagers are at times tormented by the Black Dog i.e. *depression.* You need not scamper from it by drowning yourselves in the glasses of wine, popping up sleeping pills or hiding behind the curls of smoke. Trust me, just like a real dog, the Black Dog needs to be embraced, understood, taught new tricks, and ultimately brought to heal.

My door is always open; anybody who needs to talk is always welcome. It's no good suffering in silence. I know that worse than hunger and thirst, worse than unreciprocated love, failure in exams, break-up, being unemployed, defeated or in despair... far worse than all these, is the feeling that no one, absolutely no one cares for you...

Give me a call, send me a text, come to my house, and talk to me. I always have time and will definitely hear you out. You are never alone and it'll be a pleasure if I could help in any way. There's loads of coffee, nice books, a great cook, a place for a bonfire to warm your soul and tonnes of time on my hands. I'm here for you.

I'm trying to demonstrate that someone is always listening.

*****

I shut the doors

to the clamour,

the deafening din outside

and embrace solitude.

It's the words

I find refuge in

when silence gnaws my insides.

It's where I get lost,

It's where I find myself too.

Let my words

reach those

who inwardly suffer,

find solace,

and be refurbished

for I know,

how it feels

when your heart bleeds.

Acknowledgement

I dedicate this book to -

- My loving son who happens to be mapping this dangerous territory called teenage, *without a map* ☺ - trying his best to exercise calm and helping me to maintain mine.
- All those teenagers out there, trying to chisel their dreams into realities abstaining from all enjoyments this beautiful phase of life has to offer, writing success stories.
- All those beautiful souls who could have worked miracles in the life to come, had they been alive today and not succumbed to the exam pressure. Alas! They failed to realise that the best their parents had was them.

Dear Son,

Being your parents has thrown the entire wealth of the world into our hands. You are the sun, the moon and stars to us. We are timorous parents harbouring certain trepidations like all parents do; nursing certain dreams in our fond bosoms, again, like all parents do. We are also living through your teenager years and we understand how you feel.

Life is analogous to a journey son. We all set off together full of enthusiasm; but as the journey progresses, we are beset with challenges. Many give up on the way. Others keep racing but only because they can't stop in the middle of it. They don't seem to enjoy it. They are oblivious to the beauties and challenges of the road.

It's the desire to walk that creates the path ahead.

Life is beautiful.

A beautiful life however doesn't just happen.

It is built daily by prayer, humility, sacrifices little and big, and of course hard work.

We have had face to face sessions of talks many a times, heart to heart rather. We, as parents have shared our deep anguish with you as how our hearts bleed when we hear of suicides by children whose zealot parents send them mainly for IIT JEE in search of lucrative careers.

Why can't we understand that everyone can't be an IITian or go to AIIMS?

Why do we always try to follow the rhythm set by others?

Keeping pace with others walking faster than you would soon be straining the tendons in your feet.

I advise that you respect your own rhythm.

Manage to complete your journey at your own pace.

The indecent competition plays havoc with a child's life and when her performance is not up to the mark-the result is suicide invariably with the note-'*Please forgive me Mamma, please forgive me Papa; I let you down.*'

We don't want you to kill your soul and merely be a parrot. We don't want you to become a robot solving some 5000 sums for some 1000 times just to be a good doctor or to get a nice package.

Be what you want.

Don't bother whether your tie matches your socks or not.

So what if you initially opted for Science and now you realise your call to be Humanities or something else? Go for that! You have every right to change your opinion. The world is constantly shifting. Be unapologetically contradictory as long as it causes no harm to others.

Can you make an omelette without breaking eggs?

Do what you like.

Stay healthy.

Stay happy.

Live your life to the fullest.

*****

I used to not wear any make-up.

I used to not straighten or curl my hair.

I used to have real good friends.

I used to love to go to school.

I used to not bother if I had no boy-friend.

I used to laugh a lot, and go months without crying.

I used to not care what others thought of me.

I used to think all boys were gross.

I used to think there was no such thing as love.

Damn it! I used to be happy all the time.

What happened?

*****

At seventeen I was a depressed teenager who self- harmed and now I wonder about just how painful it could possibly be to end my life...for myself, friends and above all, my family.

Right now, as I'm lying down on my couch, I can see my beautiful wife reading out a bed time story to our five-year-old making funny animal sounds.

Life does get better.

Make sure you are there to see it.

*****

Contents

Prologue

Anushka is home for a week. She has written the pre examination for AIPMT and her result is awaited. Presently she's lazing around in the house. Her Mom is on leave as she wants to spend as much time with her daughter as possible. She's watching TV.

'Omg!' she exclaims all of a sudden.

'What happened Mom?' Anushka is shocked to see her Mom look like a wrung- up mop rag.

'This is some news about...' her Mom has her eyes glued to the screen emotionless as paper.

Anushka's Dad who has been sorting out some important papers at his desk is at once drawn to the news too.

Neither of her parents utters a word.

They just gaze each other in sheer disbelief.

It's ABP news channel on.

Again some student in Kota is reported to have committed suicide.

Anushka has never talked to the guy but she does recognize her.

It's one of her seniors Amit preparing for AIPMT.

Amit's father is being interrogated for details. It's an elderly gentleman with tears of remorse in his eyes, answering...

It wasn't in the weirdest dreams of mine that my only son would commit suicide...he was a brilliant student. I'm absolutely unaware how he changed in this brief period of two years! We used to talk often though he couldn't come home whenever there was a break as he said there was lot of pressure. We didn't want him to miss anything. We'd personally visit him whenever we missed him deep. It was all fine-tuned...dunno why...' hiccups.

'...I was on a business trip when my wife called me the night ago. She made sure that I wasn't alone...that there was someone with me...I grew suspicious and the first nightmarish thought that struck my mind was...the same! ...I grew alarmed still promised her that I was able to handle the news calmly...that... she could tell.' sobs hard.

Resumes- '...all she could speak was 'Amit...shot himself.' The ground slipped from under my feet. I couldn't breathe a breath... aah! Thaa day! I had an impulse to talk to him the previous night but then thinking it was too late and he might be tired, perhaps gone to sleep...I had resisted...wish I had called! Perhaps...things might have taken a different turn then...not this for God's sake!'

'How I miss him! I feel rotten. How am I going to miss him every moment of my life! I'm not a strong woman. No more I am. I'm a vessel of glass; most vulnerable...he used to be so close to me... how could he hide things? When I'd be working in the kitchen... he'd startle me by coming in on tiptoes...and hugging me from behind. I'd pretend annoyance. I want him back! God please!' Amit's mother is bereaved.

'Would you like to tell us about the video he made just before he err...committed suicide?' the reporter asks compassionately.

'Yes when I somehow had a hold on myself, I checked his laptop to find some clues as to why did he go for such a drastic step, I was shocked to see his wallpaper. WHY DO I HAVE TO LIVE? was all that it read.' the old man breaks into uncontrollable grief.

'He'd nestle by me when five. He was a tender hearted child. He would be scared to visit the doctor, getting poked and prodded and having his blood drawn for tests. He hated syringes and medicines. How could he shoot himself? So cruel of him to have left us wailing behind!' his mother laments.

'He even made a video on his phone doing the thing! It says he felt so broken and lonely...it says, 'Dad please mujhe maaf kar dena. We could've a good future together. I could've stayed home but you *had ambition to see me at the top. I couldn't reach the top Dad! When I shoot my head with this revolver, it would slice open and you wouldn't be able to see. Still...'*

'... You might find me strong enough to tell you all this but it's the responsibility of my two daughters that keeps me alive. What father would have the heart to live on a day more having shouldered the corpse of his only son?'

'I understand.' the reporter's voice goes wet with emotion.

A brief pause.

'Would you like to say something to our youth watching this?'

'All I have to say is that if the idea of suicide strikes your mind, don't please stay alone. Come immediately in physical contact with your friends, relatives or parents at best. Better talk to them face-to-face. There's life beyond exams! Find a hobby; develop a passion that can devour your loneliness. Life is beautiful. It is precious. Amit, you haven't killed yourself. You have killed your Mom, your Dad, and your sisters whom you loved so much! Come back Amit!'

Anushka can't take any more.

She is sobbing hard.

So is her mother.

Her dad switches the television off.

The three come close enough to form a circle of love.

'Hope you...' her Dad can't give words to his apprehensions.

'Papa please! I'm a strong girl. I need not pass any tests to win your love. Do I?'

'You are the best darling! Top or not top, we love you always.'

Anushka can't still give surety if she's awake.

She wishes she wasn't.

*****

1

Gals will be Gals!

'The girl! What does she think of herself? I won't really spare her...how dare she gaze at my boy-friend to her heart's fill? Doesn't she know he is mine...and why *is...agar bhagvaan ne chaha toh* will always be mine?' Trisha seethes with frustration.

'Who the hell are you talking about?' asks Nikki.

'Simran, who else? Bloody *gavaaanrr!*' she mumbles.

'Aa-haan! And what about your dusky handsome? Was he not staring her as if would gobble her...but for your presence?' Nikki catches hold of the other side of the stick.

'I know...I won't be talking to that mongrel. His stupid heart starts flipping at the very glimpse of any better looking girl!'

'He deserves a little indifference you know...the way you generously part with your money and all for that dog's sake...' Nikki blurts out.

'I think you are right.' says Trisha knowing it is her silly teenage heart that always plays the mischief.

'Now c'mon leave it! Know what? I have got *palak-paneer* in lunch, your favourite!'

'What do you say...should I start getting my eyebrows done?' asks Trisha blinking her eyes.

'Hein?'

'Oh Madam? Where's your mind?' Trisha asks sulking.

'See I'm dying of hunger and there you are...talking of...! What's wrong with you? That *Road Roller* will have her period immediately after the lunch. You want me really to die of hunger?'

'Okay fine! Lunch first.' she giggles.

'*Lookatthm! Jus* look at him! *Lafandu!* He can never sit at a place and eat. Hee hee.' laughs Nikki pointing towards a junior boy. She is dangling her legs sitting on a felled tree trunk, an inch close to Trisha.

'*Stuppppiiid*! First finish your bite. And yes, ask your Mom to prepare the same every day. She cooks like dream! I mean it just makes my day *yaar !'*

'I will. Now...what were you asking...threading...well...don't tell me you've never gone to a parlour!' exclaims Nikki running her index finger over Trisha's eye brows.

'*Cheeee!* First wash your hands, you clumsy girl.'

'Okay okay! Never been to a...?'

'*Sachhi.* I want to *yaar* but Mom says I can't until...'

'Wait-wait-wait. The way you spoke *Mom says*...well, it reminded me of a *teenopedia* recently read- '*Mom says*...mmm...*Mom Says No Girl- Friend*!'...well u *cn* go for another book like... '*Mom Says No Eyebrows Done Until*'...heehee...silly no?'

'Shuuuuttttt up! Won't you? U know u r silly then why confirm every time?' laughs Trisha.

'Okay-okay. I'll remember next time. C'mon continue. What were you saying...?'

'...until I've cleared my tenth class. What does the concept of looking good have to do with class? She is sometimes...gosh! What to name her! Looks like she never had the desire to look good or she never had any boy-friend.' comments Trisha.

'Thuttt!' Nikki retorts.

'Guess what? The very thought of Mamma cooking alibi at home to see a boy tickles me to bones!' Trisha whispers with a wicked pleasure.

'Did aunty ever have a b.o.y.f.r.i.e.n.d? She told you? Hey! I'm having goose bumps!'

'*Tu bhi na! Jus* imagining yaar!'

'K!' she giggles.

'Painful but fact...and I know it...damn it! I don't look as good as that girl Simran does. I won't however admit that before her...E.V.E.R!!!'

'Why would you? Coz if you do, wouldn't it give her an edge over you?' Nikki adds fuel to fire, her eye balls dancing delightfully.

'You will keep all this secret no?' pleads Trisha widening her eyes.

'You trust me *naa*?' Nikki narrows hers.

'I do.' Trisha presses her hand and they jump off the tree trunk straightening their pleats.

Both walk hand in hand through the corridor of school with a wilful swing to their brown skirts. Their pony tails bounce telling the tale of forbidden joys while their flowering bodies ripple with the vigour of youth.

*****

2

Hormones Kicking into High Gear

'*Gimme* this. *Kahan se kabaadi?*' Nikki snatches the fashion magazine which Trisha carries in her school bag. Something else falls down too and so many eyes catch the sight of the little green pack- Whisper Ultra-Thin.

'*Ooooooo!!!*' a few girls exclaim blinking in delighted disbelief.

'*Sttttupiiiddd!!!*' Nikki spanks her as she bends to pick it up.

'That magazine...! I just saw Malia Obama's picture in this! Is it *ektualllly* she! Show me *naa!*'

'*Aise kaise?* I had ordered it online and have received it yesterday itself. I'll give you once I've completely gone through this.' mutters Trisha trying to cover up her embarrassment while putting the green thing back in a zip pocket this time.

'Guess what? I just love the way Malia carries herself. To my mind, she's in a unique fashion position. Whatever she wears becomes a fair game for public to discuss.' Nikki exclaims.

'Yes! And luckily she does possess a flawless understanding of how to work in that space no?' Trisha adds.

Trisha knows she isn't a kid anymore. Maybe she isn't exactly an adult woman yet but she is really ready to move on. She often worries that she isn't getting breasts like most of her friends. She is worried lest she should be the first one in the whole class to get periods or maybe the last one or...what if she got her first period right in the middle of the class and bleed right through her pants and everyone saw it...what if her pad someday fell out of her bag?

4

OMG! This was the day.

'Mom, what if I get it in the class?' she had expressed her deep most concern to her mum one day.

'If you get cramps in the class, tell the teacher you have a headache and ask to go to the nurse's office.'

'And what am I to tell the nurse?' Trisha had asked foolishly.

'Tell the nurse the truth of-course, but you don't have to announce to the whole class that you have menstrual cramps.'

...

Periods. Acne. Body-odour. Unwanted hair.

And...much more.

Those are the biggies every girl in the class is wondering about. Nikki is very conscious about her looks. She has recently been hit by the hormone misbehaviour that causes acne. She's been using acne cleanser, toner moisturiser, oil free sunscreen and what not! She's even been to a dermatologist secretively. She's been in floods of tears coz she thinks her legs are stumpy. When she confessed this to her mom, her mom didn't know whether to laugh or cry. Laugh at her inhibitions coz to everyone else it's pretty obvious that she has beautifully long and slim legs. Cry coz God knows why is it the contrary she sees in the mirror.

The celebrity culture and the rise of image obsessed social media are having a big impact on the way youngsters see themselves.

One third of female teens feel urged to look like celebrities and wouldn't stop from contemplating even extreme measures like surgery to change their appearance.

Whereas in boys' case, CASUALS ARE COOL. Shirts maybe hot, but Tees are goddamn awesome. They'll fit into anything that's loose and comfy. What they care for is latest gadgets. Be it laptops, phones or headphones, they're geeks. They yearn for cars. CARS ARE BIG BOYZ' TOYZ – Audis, Bimmers, Lambos and Jags – their eyes as if feast on 'em. These gadgets can absorb their fertile brains for hours at a stretch!

...

A short, plump teacher with small kohled eyes enters the class. Usually she wears *salwar-kameez* unrelieved even by the thinnest border and always attempting to look professional and severe. Today however she's wearing a fearsome green sari with embroidery done three decades ago perhaps. Her skin tone looks brighter in the colour. Her hair usually pleated so tight that not a single strand dares come out, has been pulled back in a neat bun and that too rose bedecked! No oil today. It looks like it is her golden jubilee of marriage or something.

Nikki springs at once as she finds others standing.

Trisha is humming and leafing through the magazine still sweetly unmindful of the nudge from Nikki.

'Hey you! *Maharani* Trisha. Don't you have the manners to wish your teacher? *Pairon mein mehandi lagai hai kya?'* asks *Road Roller*...oops! Their Hindi teacher.

'I...I am so sorry ma'am. I didn't notice.' Trisha tucks her favourite strands of hair behind her ear.

'Always posing to be Aishvarya Rai! Moving around with senior boys! That too- the most notorious ones! As if we don't know anything...' the teacher shoots her a soured look before turning towards the blackboard, her small heels skittering on the marble floor.

'Bachhan ma'am! Aishvarya Bachhan...*shaadi ke baad*. And those are good boys.' Trisha speaks with a sassy smile.

'Thanks for the correction sweetheart!!!' the teacher is indeed bamboozled at the display of insolence.

Whoops and moan break out from the class. Trisha and Nikki are on the verge of whooping too but they contain themselves. The entire bunch of mischievous ones indulges in whispers and gasps, nudges and did-you-see-that looks while the teacher's pets ogle in disbelief.

'Ask your Dad to get you admitted to some modelling agency. You won't have to curb your desire of bringing your beautiful locks to limelight then.'

'But...ma'am...*aaj toh aapne bhi lat nikali hui hai*...anything special today?' asks the daring Trisha, feeling like a queen by the attention she's getting.

The teacher is too shocked to utter a word further.

She immediately manages to bring the host of unruly tendrils that has escaped the bun, to discipline.

'*Baba!* This girl *toh!* How do your parents tolerate this cheekiness?'

Trisha sulks while the class has its fill of the daily comedy.

'The woman!' Trisha utters between clenched teeth, incandescent with outrage.

Nikki comforts her through understanding eyes and Trisha slides back into the seat once again, heart hammering in agitation.

Now her lips move soundlessly and her fingernail digs at the table top.

*****

3

If not actually Love... may be...a Deep Liking

'Why so upset, *haan?*' asks Ronny.

'*Tu mujhe haath mat lagana, bol deti hun!*' Trisha's eyes simmer with resentment and humiliation.

Ronny, in an effort to calm her down holds her by shoulders. She convulses in anger. Oops! The top button of her school shirt rolls down somewhere near the classroom door. Thank God! All but the two have left for the games period.

He bends on all fours looking for the button and finds it at last behind the door.

He knows not that Trisha stands right over his head with her teary eyes digging the floor for the same.

Naturally enough, he bumps into her as he unbends.

The glossy elastic strap of her teenage bra is visible on her left shoulder.

His crazy heart races with excitement.

'Ouch! You fool!' One of her hands reaches her head to press where she's hurt.

Ronny doesn't mind the insult. He's used to.

He actually burns with a sudden desire to have her buttery skin shoulders in his grab.

Trisha at once drops her stiff manner checking her desire for even she has always yearned for one such personal moment with Ronny.

Perhaps after a kiss he'd be all hers...

Perhaps he wouldn't be craving for Nancy then...like...she feels he sometimes does...

She fixes her luminous eyes on him for a while deciding on the right words with which to soften her resentment.

'Oops! I'm so sorry Trisha. It was an accident and by the way... you should have stood at some distance *yaar! Ab maaf bhi kar de!'* he mops his brows as he hisses vehemently *kuch bolegi bhi?'*

And there comes a husky whisper-'I like you!'

'!!!' there is something breath stopping about the way she has spoken these words.

She gives him no time to react. Getting hold of her shirt collars she dashes for the staffroom hoping that some kind teacher might have a needle and a thread.

Ronny looks d.r.u.n.k.

He touches his wrist and feels that his pulse jumps crazily.

'*Gals r strainge*! Means she really likes me! My relationship status on Facebook immediately needs to be updated! Umm...I'm feeling wonderful! Ronny dear you are finally in Love! Well...if not actually Love...at least you are in a really deep Liking. You have met the most amazing girl and you totally NEED to go out with her.' he mutters under breath piercing through the crowd of students like an arrow and makes his way to the playground.

...

Trisha's palms go sweaty, stomach churning; her mind occupied with how vulnerable does she go vis-à-vis Ronny!

She moves towards the school bus smitten with a pang of longing...so sharp that the pain of love is almost physical.

...

The bus, bloated with noisy students edges its way out of the school premises as it waits for a few teachers who haven't still turned up. Trisha has positioned herself comfortably, sweetly unmindful that she's blocking off the others who are yet to board, unmindful of their angry comments as well.

There are stray dogs on the road side barking up a storm.

Trisha tangled in her own thoughts, is finally perturbed by their blood curdling yowls.

She takes her revenge by wrinkling up her nose at them in disdain.

The dogs let out angry yelps.

She evens the score finally by murmuring-*doggies kahin ke!*

Smiles within.

She prefers the frilly oblivion rewinding the scene in her mind how she bumped into her dream guy a few periods ago, a.n.d. what lovely sensation it was when he stared her so closely.

*****

4

Let's Dance Mommy!

'We were both young when I first saw you...

I close my eyes

And the flashback starts...

I see, you make your way through the crowd

And say hello...ooo...'

'Helllloooo!!! Anybody home???' Trisha croons.

'Nobdy home!' her mother croons back in response, smiling and pushing the glass door open.

Trisha flings her school shoes aside and plays the music system at a loud volume.

'Mom what's there for lunch and by the way how did your party go?' Trisha pulls the rubber band off her hair and runs fingers through the dense bunch.

'Ummm...it was manchurian, biryani, aloo-dum and...malai-kofta and stuffed nans.'

'My mouth begins watering. Left some?' Trisha yells from the dining hall tying her hair again. She looks herself in the mirror swaying to the song.

'Yes yes. And...*My Miss World*...again you left your tiffin on the study table!'

'Ummm...so silly I am!' she carefully puts her school bag on a chair and wraps it with her maroon blazer, smiles at it whimsically and twitches it saying 'that's like a good boy!'

11

Next she directly heads for the kitchen unfastening her pony tail again.

'Make it quick or your *Miss World* will die of hunger.' she picks up a few onion rings and cucumber's and begins munching.

'Leave it! First wash your hands.' Ragini, her Mom, slaps her hand.

'For God's sake! Stop treating me like a kid!' Trisha roars like a wounded tigress throwing the rings in the bin directly.

'What's wrong with you?' Ragini asks; her eyes boring into Trisha's.

Trisha takes a deep breath, regains her composure and smiles.

'Nothing. I'm fine. Okay fine. I'm in no mood to argue. Let's... let's do what...let's dance!' she fastens her pony tail again.

'Let's what?' Ragini gives a short, mirthless laugh.

'Let's dance Mom!' Trisha eases the air by extending a warm smile that really overwhelms Ragini.

'A.n.d. you really think you have grown up darling?' Ragini asks, stuffing her mouth with a few slices of cucumber.

'Mom please!'

'Trisha please! I'll fall down. Look at my waist. I can't d.a.n.c.e.'

'You can! I'll teach you. Now c'mon!' she pulls her out in the dining hall and rewinds the song *Nashe Si Chadh Gayi.*

Her Mom looks at her, intrigued.

'Now listen! Pay attention to the dance-step timing and the beats.' her neck has already started swaying in rhythm. She pulls out a natural rose bud from the vase and clenches it between her sparkling white rows of teeth.

Ragini doubles with mirth.

'Don't laugh Mom. You'll be playing the girl. K?'

'Ummm...k!'

12

Trisha rolls off the rubber-band from her pony tail one more time and flings it in the air.

'Hey! It's me playing the girl! How come you have hair longer than mine?' Ragini shakes back her hair.

'*Ye aaj kal ka ladka hai.* Hee-hee. Even Shahrukh Khan has a pony tail and yes! Sonu Nigam too!'

Ragini throws herself on Trisha's tender shoulders with almost a rude jerk.

'Ouch! Mom!'

'I told you, I can't!'

'I told you, you can! Let's try again. Wait a minute. We'll use this a little later.' She shoves the rose stem into the vase again.

'Some other number, maybe, we should try. Now hold my finger. Yes. And one arm behind you. Clear? You have to twirl but please don't squeeze my finger the same clumsy way...'

Ragini nods like a child suppressing her smiles.

'No sentiment without the rose s.o. plz if you don't mind...' Trisha giggles.

She helps her Mom to bend, to twirl, to rest her body on her slender arms telling her to close her eyes with a passionate smile.

Ragini can't hold any more.

She laughs like never before, her waist aching though.

'Expressions Mom! Where are the expressions?' Trisha exclaims, her eyes twinkling with an untold joy.

'Stop all this now! Ho! I can't...I can't.'

Both fall onto bed, laughing.

'I'm feeling so hungry that I can devour anything. You know what our Sanskrit teacher used to quote? *Bubhukshtim kim na karoti* something- something...which means...a hungry person can commit any sin...hee-hee...*dekha mujhe abhi bhi yaad hai...*'

Ragini is all breathless and sweating mid-winter months.

She comes to the kitchen all wheezing yet gets busy in serving lunch.

'Mom, what's this? It's all so oily and spicy! I can't eat this.'

'Where's the oil dear? I do try my best to avoid excess of oil in food.'

'Ho! If you guys d.i.e.t. like this, you can never have the tyres off your waist.' Trisha laughs a cynical laughter.

'Look at your manners!' Ragini barks, burning with humiliation and heartache.

Trisha stops eating, casts an angry glance at Mom and makes way for the basin.

...

Trisha gets on Ragini's nerves really.

...

Trisha yearns for a reassuring hug from her Mom which she rarely gets these days. What she gets the most from her is finger-pointing, pricking-comments, hurting-comparisons and mocking-smiles at how incompetent she is. May be she isn't as good a girl as her Mom used to be, back in her teenage or as studious as Anushka is but then she expects unconditional love from her Ma and Pa so that she might again feel pampered, loved and more fulfilled a person. She can't of course fall on her knees and ask for a motherly kiss, a nurturing hug from her father or a pat on her back from the teacher whenever she does well.

...

'Yeah! You've got the point now! I have no manners. I have no manners mom! ...cuz you never seem to have time to teach me some...cuz you are enjoying the juicy gossips with your frns... social circle you know...cuz you are squandering money in clubs, kitty parties and parlours...giggling and gorging on titbits leaving the previous night's food for us to feed upon...' Trisha bites back with 'go-to-hell' nonchalance, hooks her thumbs into her school bag straps and rushes towards the staircase fuming.

Ragini is standing in the doorway tears springing to her eyes and lips buttoned.

...

An hour passes by.

...

The mother has her daily dose of siesta.

...

The daughter orders a Cheese Burst Pizza and has it in her room.

...

Dear Diary

4.05 PM

We won't be talking about Mom right now. At night we will.

Here's what's been happening recently. Amy, my classmate went out with Neel, then they broke up- well she actually got dumped by him. But then she started going out with another guy from class twelfth but then... he started two- timing her with another girl from his own class. Neel decided next that he liked me. Me! He then decided he didn't fancy me! But then I told him I liked him too. I ACTUALLY WENT OUT WITH HIM! Wow! I actually did it! This is how it happened:

Neel: 'Hello, can I speak to xxx?'

Maid: 'Yes, hang on.'

Neel: 'Er hi, xxx it's me Neel.'

Me: 'Er hi.'

Neel: 'Er...xxx, will u go out wd me?'

Me: 'Yeah.'

*****

5

The Roller-Coaster Ride

'Have been to parlour darling? Why, your face shines like anything!' compliments Akshay as he kisses Ragini's cheek setting down his bag at the door and dropping his coat.

'*Arrey kahan!* I'm not getting any time for that. Look at my hair! I was to go for the second session of hair spa. *Vaise achcha yaad dilaya tumne*...lemme get tomorrow's appointment from my beautician on phone.'

'Sure!' a boyish grin splits open Akshay's face.

'How is our princess Trisha doing?' asks Akshay rolling off his socks. 'She's fine. Gets edgy sometimes though.'

'Teenage sweetheart! Teenage! Remember our first kiss in the school canteen?'

'Oh shut up! You start any time!' Ragini blushes.

'She is getting spoilt I tell you. Whenever I talk of etiquette, she throws a damn *you-don't–know-anything* look. I am scared sometimes.'

'Are you? No need to be. She is our doll! She has inherited this temperament from us. I think we need to be a little more patient. Patience is the key darling.' Akshay advises accepting the glass of water offered.

'You'll always teach me...not your daughter? She is happier with her friends outside and at home it is either her laptop or her diary.'

'You know what Ragini? *Part of adolescence is about separating and individuating. These teenagers need to separate from their parents in order to find themselves.*'

'As if we didn't undergo this phase! We were never rude to our parents.' Ragini rants, her default state whenever she's besieged by guilt.

'Ours was a different age honey! It was not an age of Internet, Facebook, Google, Twitter and Smartphones! These influences matter a great deal in moulding their mental world.'

'Whatever! And why should I keep pampering her if she doesn't need me except when the fit of fancy is on and she wants me as her dance partner?'

'Dance partner! Sounds interesting! C'mon darling! *Responding to a teenager by returning rejection is a mistake. She needs her mother whether she admits or not. She is on a roller coaster. You need to stand by her as a firm post she can count on...yes, whenever she needs. All you need to do is to weather this teenage rebellion with perfect calm.'* Akshay wisely explains.

'It's all big talk Akshay! So easy to say!' Ragini wipes her tears.

'By letting her know that you are there for her...no matter what...she may let down her guard someday and...confide in you. Believe me! I'll talk to her. Does that make my beautiful wife happy?' he cuddles her.

'I'm feeling too tired. These parties are sometimes too boring no? I think you shouldn't talk to her right now. She doesn't let anybody enter her room when she is sulking.'

'Did she have dinner?'

'Dinner. Yes.'

'Serve me dinner fast so that I can serve you love after that.' Akshay pinches her waist.

'Shut up!' blushes Ragini.

*****

6

Mood Swings...

I am feeling very weepy today. I suffer from low self-esteem. None bothers however. You know what? These elders don't understand us at all and then they pretend to be caring. Caring, my foot! They want to treat us like kids. *'Wash your hands first!'* *Batao!*

Wise people say there's no wrong that a good conversation can't fix. Our matters get worse after a conversation! If I hoist the flag of freedom, all hell breaks loose! I do want freedom; freedom from their bloody dos and don'ts; freedom to wear what I want. You know what? Our teachers are no less than our mothers. They make it a point...that our skirts should be fixed a little above the bellybutton a.n.d. must reach beneath knees! *Seriously!*

Know what?

I was kinda quivering with a pleasant pain when his eyes rested on my...the pain tore me to shreds as if...I...I would have kissed him there and then...had it not been in school...he is...he is so... so magnetic *yaar!*

AND I have lot of iron elements inside perhaps...hee-hee...

Know what?

I told him!

I told him that I liked him!

He hasn't officially said that he likes me too but umm...I sense something like that. We have kissed in dreams many a times but what actually happens is that I'm in an agonizing state of mind whenever I face him. The butterflies in my stomach go so crazy at the very sight of his. I can barely formulate words. He walks into the class, and I can't jus'...stop...staring. I try to work up the nerve to talk to him but freak out every time.

Let's see...

I'd have waited for him to say that first but then that girl you know, Nancy I told u abt...she's after him!

So I went against my grain.

Hope u understand.

Chill pill! I don't kind of DIE ON HIM!!! Jus' time pass *yaar*!

I know there will be many more.

This jus' the beginning...

Tomorrow is Anushka's Bday.

We are gonna have blast.

So what if I don't like her?

I can't really like her as long as...she doesn't stop topping the class; as long as... she doesn't stop pretending to be so disciplined in her typical oily plaits and long skirts; as long as...she doesn't start enjoying the wicked pleasures we do; as long as...the Road Roller doesn't some-day make her a butt of ridicule as she makes me daily...as long as...this girl doesn't some-day shock everyone by saying that...mmm...that she doesn't know the answer...!!! Hee Hee!

That will never happen. I know. *Book worm jo hai.* I HATE HER!!!

But you know what?

Ronny is also coming to the party.

Does that make clear why should I tolerate her?

Gd ni8sss...

Trisha forgives her Mom remembering those good times when her Mommy sat up whole nights rubbing her back, giving medication, keeping wet rags on her burning forehead and caressing her when the obstinate fever wouldn't just break. She can't forget those times. Those times make her give her Mom another chance and then another till the chances ran out one bad day.

'I love you Mom!' Trisha murmurs snuggling under the red satin comforter that she loves so much.

*****

7

No Shopping with Mom for God's Sake!

Trisha is at Nikki's.

For the party plans of course.

Nikki loves all those glossy fashion magazines. Since the day her eyes fell on one, she's devoured all written words as she has an insatiable appetite for all things fashion. Out of her desire to fuel her fire online and connect with a new audience, she's recently taken up writing blog. She's a fan of teenagers' blogs like *Birdie Wears a Tie, A Bent Piece of Wire, Collie's Street Chic etc.*

'Shopping. The very word excites me so much. Don't you like shopping?' asks Nikki.

'Hey! I do like shopping but I resent time spent in shopping. It is sheer waste of life when one can be listening to an iPod in the room and relaxing.'

An attitude that perfectly captures the teen blend of vehemence and torpor.

'You know what? Mom is always going mad about shopping. *Chalo na* Trisha. It'll be fun. Fun my foot! You know what? I suggested well humouredly that I was ready to go shopping with her if she be willing to be charged hundred rupees per-ten-minute she made me shop. Hee hee.'

'OMG!' exclaims Nikki popping her pink bubble-gum.

'Hee hee.'

'She must've slapped u no, u girl?'

'No! She's an intriguing mix of contradictions. She said, 'No big deal. Okay.' Trisha imitates her Mom.

'Really?' Nikki ogles in disbelief.

'Yesss!' Trisha is impatient to share more.

'Then then?' Nikki is impatient to know more.

...

(Neuroscientists say there's a massive rewiring job going on in a teen's mind and that to grow best it needs to experience and seek novelty.

A mother wants to help her daughter shying of her changing body into clothes that might boost her confidence.

Ragini insists buying things for Trisha for she knows the teen agers trends these days. Many a tantrums go on in the changing rooms otherwise, if girls go shopping on their own.

Ragini however is painfully aware that *it's her credit card that is wanted, not an opinion.)*

...

Ideally a mother's role would be similar to the one on the touch line. She should make sure that her daughter gets to the match, offer advice if asked, support her, cheer her on but she shouldn't actually try to play the game for her daughter.

Of course there will be misses, defeats and fouls along the way but she has to stand back and let them happen.

...

...

'Well, I'd love to do show-rooming or reverse- show-rooming *kinda* shopping like many of our friends do...but my mother, *The Supreme Court* you know, would surely sign-off on every purchase I make.' Trisha sulks.

'Eighteen is a cool number you know. You can't have a credit card of your own till then. So...enjoy shopping with your Mom.' teases Nikki.

'But it gets embarrassing like hell when you need to buy something for the first time in your life. Say for example...I needed a bra.'

'You needed what?' Nikki gawks in utter disbelief.

'A bra! As simple as that! I have started filling out in the boob area. Some girls in our class have already made the move. Now please don't behave typical as if you'll never need one. *'Trisha used to be our best friend. Until she bought a bra.'* Hope this isn't going to be doled out to me. And for God's sake stop ogling me like an owl.' blurts out Trisha.

'How did you know? I mean how did you guess you needed one?'

'Have been trying different things. Had read somewhere about the pencil test you know - positioning a pencil between your breasts and pushing them together. If the pencil stays put, you need a bra.' whispers Trisha with an all knowing air.

'Haan!'

'I know you are going to try the thing tonight.' winks Trisha. 'Now, as the story goes, my Mom wants me to buy a bra which is not for the most part, overly sexual.'

'And what do you want?'

'I want one that screams 'sex.''

'Tu pagal ho gayee hai?'

'I hate Nancy for her big boobs. I want to draw that bloody Ronny to me.'

'Aah! But what I feel you know...you shouldn't have to buy a sequined push-up bra when fifteen-sixteen. You shouldn't have to feel pressurized to look a certain way a woman would. BTW it must have been an awkward conversation no?' Nikki asks.

'*Euhghhh!* It was a heinously awkward chat with Mom. She was like pleasantly shocked. She looked so proud of me. I died inside. Her gaze settled on my tiny boobs.'

'So embarrassing! You must have felt rotten!'

'She took me to our nearest department store.'

'Sometimes being a teen makes you want to die.'

'Yeah right. I prayed no one I knew would be there. OMG! THERE WERE SO MANY BRAS! I told Mum I didn't want to be there anymore. Like I had said something illegitimate, she threw an angry glance at me and then whispered something to the female store keeper. That girl, the store keeper asked me what type of bra I wanted!'

'Oh Jesus!'

'I said...I *dunno.* I don't care.' I picked up the very first one I saw, feeling so embarrassed. 'Perhaps you could start with a training bra.' she suggested. And I was like...close to tears. And next... Mum pushed me into the changing room and brought one tape measure.'

'Awww!'

'Take off your top.' she directed. I was like...oh hell! Why did I tell her I wanted one?'

'And no one's seen your boobs before. Mmm...what if they are not normal? What does normal mean anyway?' Nikki adds, giggling.

'Exactly. Now she started talking numbers which I didn't understand. 'Does that feel the right size?' she asked. HOW THE HELL WOULD I KNOW? We went back to the shop floor. It was like...evybdy was staring at my teeny tiny boobs. They knew exactly what we had been doing inside. They were nudging and laughing. The joke was...'me'.

'So...after all that possible embarrassment, you got what you want. How does it feel?' Nikki twitches her upper arm.

'Ouch! As soon as I got home and tried that new bra...I hated it. The straps kept falling down. The top kept bunching up underneath. Don't ever buy one! Okay? IT ITCHES SO MUCH!!! I took it off. Bye-Bra-Bye.'

'And...w.h.a.t. a.b.o.u.t. R.o.n.n.y?' Nikki mischievously asks, hunched on a small stool at her feet painting her toenails a shiny chocolate brown.

'*Leddhim* go to hell. Hee hee.'

'Hee hee.'

*****

8

Fun, Festive Spirits and the Mayhem

A grand hotel.

Two wheelers are throbbing, waiting to be parked.

Many guys and gals are seen hi-fiving, giggling, cheeping, waving and kissing absolutely unmindful of others.

A few cars are crawling towards the huge entrance.

The parents are seen dropping their wards and making sure it is the right place. They look anxiously keen on having a look what kind of gentry invited while their handsome sons-n-pretty daughters sulk to see their Moms and Dads linger on.

HAPPY BIRTHDAY ANUSHKA the banner shows them in.

All faces scintillating in the shimmering lamp shades.

The gals who look most unpretentious in their school uniforms are looking no less than models walking on the ramp with their made up faces, glossed up lips and waxed legs.

Guys are adorned with killing smiles and hair gelled standing in spikes. They are seen texting on their latest mobile phones. They are exuding expensive perfumes and after-shaves and an indefinable aura of romance. But you can still find some dudes that are hanging out in their informal trousers and tees with super-intelligent quotes written thereon like *'Save Water, Drink Beer.'*(That's some great advice!) This unmindful, cool-ass style gets them more girls than those well-attired 'gentlemen'.

'Looking gorgeous *yaar!*' exclaims Trisha.

'Sachh?' asks Aliya, her class mate.

'*Muucch!*' Trisha replies.

'*Muaah*! I could die out of joy!' a kiss planted as a token of thanks. Their friendship bumped up several notches atonce.

'Where be the *budday* gal?'

'Over there.'

'Her Mom-Dad aren't going to come, I suppose?'

'Well, I don't think so...or you could've seen them holding her arm like she was a three year birthday girl hee-hee.'

'Yeah right! These parents first bring their wards up and then wish to smother them by their reassuring cuddles that they love...'

'Hee-hee.' Trisha laughs her customarily silly laughter.

'Hiiii!!!! You look kinda h.o.t. *yaar*! I never knew pink suits you *thisss* much!' Nancy compliments Trisha.

'Do I? Well, thanks dear. Umm...no guys gonna join us? A boring party?' Trisha looks pretty heartened by the compliments.

'Look there! There's the one ur eyes are hunting for.' Nancy beckons.

Trisha bites her lips drinking in the sight of Ronny.

'How the girl behaves...like...like she were not...*a*...!' Trisha indulges in monologue.

'All the best!' whispers Nancy.

'How come that...?'

'We have had a break off. The spell broken, kind of...now you may enjoy the *despo.*'

'Ohh! It isn't my birthday but then it certainly is no less than a gift. Thanks haan!'

'*U r wlcm*. Now since I have left him for you, when do you plan to do the r.e.a.l. z.i.n.g. t.h.i.n.g. with him?'

'Shut up!'

'Why shut up? We have had it a number of times. He is awesome that way...I tell you haan.'

'OMG! Don't tell me! When? Where?' her stomach cramps.

'At my home!'

'Don't tell me!!!'

'I'm telling...you know? It was between 3.00 and 6.00 p.m.-the unsupervised hours. That's the time when we are back from school and our parents aren't back from their respective offices. Simple!'

'OMG!'

'Do you plan to die a...virgin?' laughs Nancy.

'No! But I don't think it's cool to have sex at this age. I'm into sports and I love to hang out with friends, at the movies and the malls. That's it. I don't wanna take a chance of pregnancy tests and all...the humiliation of having such a big secret out!! Can't imagine!'

'Looks like you've never been offered.'

'I have been! But I think virginity is an important thing which I don't want to lose. I will do it but on the right time, the right place and with the right kind of a guy...'

'So Ronny is not...'

'No way! He's jus' a guy friend.'

'Worthy enough for a kiss or not even that? Why the hell have you been so desperate to have him then?'

'Shhh! Kiss will do. You know...' both share naughty glances and it looks like they have been the best of the friends ever.

'OMG! I'll die laughing!' Trisha is all bubbly like a spring gushing.

'Die if you want but first do the r.e.a.l...'

'Z.i.n.g. t.h.i.n.g. right?'

'Well, let's first wish Anushka.'

'Sure. I'll join you.'

'Anushka...Anushka...I'm so happy for you. I mean WE ARE so happy for you. Wish u a *verrrry happppy baddddey!*' Both kiss her and extend the gifts which they apparently don't want to carry any more especially Nancy who is wearing a sari for the first time in her life.

Nancy is rather plump as compared to Trisha's delicate zero figure that she would love to maintain.

Anushka looks soberly beautiful in her full sleeved black evening gown. She is wearing a gold chain with a beautiful little gold pendant gifted by her Mom today. Her dense hair falls up to her waist in utmost glory. A divine glow rests on her face.

'Look at her hair!' whispers Nancy.

'Yeah...like...by some magic the oily pleats overnight turned into such a rippling sheet of lovely hair!'

'Yes but otherwise looking so simple...I mean...umm...you know what I mean.'

'Hee-hee. Know what? Even her Mum would've looked the same in the dress she wears.'

'Perhaps. Know what? She reminds me of a nun...a.l.w.a.y.s...*a nun who has no fun*-sort of.' says Nancy in cherry voice.

'*Haan?*' Trisha's eyes twinkle.

'By God! *Tu bhi naa!*' both chortle.

Ronny wears a pair of faded jeans with a blue checked shirt, Reebok shoes, a thick gold chain in the neck, his shirt partially unbuttoned. He is playing with his car's keys.

'Still annoyed?' he asks Trisha in the most sensuous voice.

'*Naa re!* I was *ekchually* dying to see you!' Trisha can see the hollow at his neck, the tanned, taut skin below.

He wears an iron stud in his ear. His eyes glint in a way as to send a shiver of excitement down her spine. She allows him to pull her leisurely towards the dance floor.

'Really?' he winks, his eyes caressing her moist lips.

'Really.' she giggles rolling her eyes and letting his arm rest on her shoulders.

'Don't tell me! You've come by your own car?' she asks with sparkles in her eyes.

'*Wanna* have long drive?' asks Ronny running his fingers in his hair which she notices has grown a little longer...curling crisply at the edge of his collar.

'I'd love to but some other day.'

'Read of some looming accident in your daily horoscope or what? *Abhi chalte hein naa.Kya kahti hai?*' he pokes her in the ribs.

'I don't read such things! *Cheeee!*' Trisha suppresses her lovely dimples.

'What do you read? Ummm...by the way...have you read E.l.e.v.e.n. M.i.n.u.t.e.s.?' his Adam's apple bobbing up and down in excitement.

'Not yet.'

'Do it.' he sings leisurely.

'Sure.' Trisha who doesn't give an extra edge to anyone, dotes on him as though he were some magician who held her spellbound.

She gushes on and on at him pretending to hang onto his each word.

The party explodes onto the dance floor.

'Don't Let Me Down...'

Everybody is enjoying.

...

It is the very first of its kind a party for Anushka where her parents aren't there. She is missing them and texting them to reach the spot soon.

A few guys beckon Ronny and he immediately nods an understanding nod, makes an excuse and moves out of the dance floor.

'Where...?' Trisha tries to hold him back to her.

'I'll be back in a few minutes' a flying kiss is bounced towards her that she pretends to catch.

She wears a long babe pink dress with lots of frills around the shoulders. The frills keep kissing her delicious cheeks in between propped by the air that wafts in every time the door opens. She shakes out her hair and is very light on her feet. By the way she has had her threading done...the first time...looking pretty superior...

Nancy is on the dance floor with other guys-n-gals. Her buttery frame is draped in spangled silk the colour of onion skin. Her *sari ka pallu* which she has teamed with tiny golden pearls sweeps the dance floor in between, slipping off her shoulders.

She is really enjoying the moment.

No residues of a recent break-off visible on her face.

She is dancing crazily on the crazy beats of the song 'Dil Cheez Tujhe De di...'

Paramdeep, the most notorious boy of class twelfth, is found taking liberties with her. He looks literally drunk. Nancy doesn't seem to mind his coming close to her or taking any liberties with her hair or *pallu.*

The next track is a mixed beat but they all beautifully change the steps accordingly. Nancy takes such nice dance steps! Her hair swirls beautifully with every move. It looks like she were a wave of wind twirling delightfully. Since Nancy has taken a few sips of the soft drink offered by Paramdeep, her head has somewhat started spinning. As the song dies down to welcome yet another, she takes a staggering step backward and a hand comes up at-once to steady her. Of course from Paramdeep who in a fit of impulse holds Nancy by her fleshy waist and implants a passionate kiss on her lips.

Trisha can't believe this!

A day ago or two she was after Ronny and...the girl!

A certain twelfth class guy flees from the spot and brings back Ronny with a few more guys who pull Paramdeep down the dance floor holding him by his collars.

'*Haramjjjade!* Don't you know she's my date?' screams Ronny.

'She was. Ho-hai Nancy! You didn't tell the bastard you have had a recent crush on me?'

Nancy is apparently too shocked to utter a word.

She clings on to Paramdeep showing her latest preference.

'You girl! You always loved me, no?' yells Ronny venomously.

'But now you love Trisha, right?' dimples flash in her plump cheeks.

Trisha is embarrassed beyond words.

Paramdeep twirls a lock of Nancy's hair between his fingers with an air of defiance.

'Get your hand off I say or...'

'Or what you rascal...?'

'I'm gonna kill you!'

'Kill me then...c'mon! Kill me! *Dar gaya kya?*' Paramdeep slaps him.

Enraged, Ronny and his friends, all drunk, attack him. They are making a great unnecessary din.

Trisha intervenes but she is pushed aside by Ronny.

She regrets her impulsiveness. She sobs; her face turning from flame to ash. She has her lower lip ragged as she has unknowingly been chewing on it, her default expression when tensed.

Anushka, horrified, rushes to the reception and makes a call.

By the time the receptionist reaches the spot, it is a pool of blood around Paramdeep and he is found crumpled in a heap.

Nancy, too scared to stand by him any-more, hurries out of the party hall, all silken hustle and urgent bustle. Her cheeks flush in shame...or may be it is the fear that has better of hers...she starts her Activa and is off to home.

Ronny rushes to pick his metallic wrist band lying on the floor with which he hit Param. His eyes are teary and he can't find it.

Trisha hands him over the band with the new born hatred in her eyes.

She has had too much today.

All that she misses right now is a big empty page of her diary even more than a '*not- to-worry-Sweet*' hug from her parents.

Anushka rushes to hug her Mom. Apparently she is too shocked to say anything. Her father gives her an assuring hug with 'we'll take care' kind of look in his eyes.

'Daddy, I didn't even invite Paramdeep.' she is trying to formulate her thoughts into coherence but fails.

'I'm sure you have no hand in the mess. Stay calm.' says Anushka's Mom.

'Had there been my parents, they'd have slapped me without making an inquiry ...for...for they don't trust me the same perhaps...' thinks Trisha dolefully.

They immediately lift the still bleeding Paramdeep in their arms and put him in their car to be taken to the hospital.

...

...

He's had several stitches near his left eye.

The wounds will pass.

Scars would remain.

A jab of regret.

The marks of wrong doing.

Moreover both Ronny and Param have been detained from writing the impending Board Examination.

Anushka has resolved within to wash her hands off such class-mates who may give her ill fame. She wouldn't allow them to bring stigma to the self-esteem her parents enjoy in the society.

Moreover she has to pass class tenth with flying colours if she has to fulfil her dream of being someone in the crowd.

Trisha is on lookout for some other guy.

Ronny?

Ronny is a forgotten dream. ☺

BTW what exactly did the 'zing thing' mean?

The two words swoosh around in her head for long...

Fantasies flit through her mind...

*****

9

Patching the Mess Up

Ronny is seen in the school canteen with many others lined up at the window. He can't really stand in the queue and wait. There are juniors he can bully. The nice aroma of *chola-kulchaas* and *samosas* plays mischief all around. It isn't a canteen spacious enough to sit and eat. There are however marble slabs outside occupied mostly by girls chatting, ogling and giggling a.l.w.a.y.s.

Too much of girlie stuff!

Ronny has tried to make up with Trisha because somehow he feels she is his type of girl- foot-loose and fancy-free. He'd sent her a beautiful broad butted bottle of perfume with an offer for a long drive in his new car but she's bluntly refused it saying she's too sober a girl to go out with him.

'Please don't send me again for errands like this. Your Trisha is too much of attitude! Take your perfume back and let me go.' pleads one of Ronny's friends thrusting the cute bottle in his hand.

'Why have you brought it here in school, man? What if the *khadoos Principal* comes for a random check again...?'

'What do I care?' the later shrugs his shoulders with pure unconcern.

'What do you care *haan?'* Ronney catches hold of his earlobes.

'Ouch! *Dukhta hai yaar! Arram se!'* the skin behind his ears is hot and reddened.

'Look! He's having perfume! Ho!' one of the girls indicates.

'Awww! It must be for his latest chick. *Tu use janti hai?'*

'No idea!' more of sniggering, ribbing.

35

'*Get an idea!*' the entire bunch of girls bursts into an uncontrollable laughter.

'What *khee-khee* you stupids! Uff!' Ronny barks.

The girls are subdued at once.

'Who does the girl think she is!' he mutters between clenched teeth.

'Looks like some girl has rejected his gift, he swooned over.' whispers a girl.

The others shush her and flee the spot still tsk-tsking.

Ronny flings the bottle in the bushes and his *samosas* too.

'*Bhaiya!* The bottle hasn't broken yet for I heard no shattering sound. May I take it?' asks a junior flatteringly.

'Of course yes! Who do you want to gift it any ways?' chuckles Ronny.

'Well...she is Priyanka...she puts on nice fragrances daily. I think...'

'Good going *haan!*' he cocks his head to one side and laughs.

*****

10

Writing a Success Story

Vyom

'Take some rest son. At least straighten out the kinks in your back. Almost half the night is gone.' Vyom's father advises, concerned.

Vyom is a brilliant guy with perfect record of academics till date. Currently he is preparing for UPSC exam. Food, health and recreation are trivialities that he can't spare time for. With limited number of attempts allowed, and nearly five to six lakh applicants taking the exam each year out of which only approximately 1,000 or less make the cut, it is one of the toughest exams to crack.

He's been disconnected from the world outside for a number of months and strangely enough he seems to have got pretty used to this seclusion.

'I'm okay Dad! You may go and sleep.'

'Are you sure dear?'

'*No yessss!*' answers Vyom, a playful smile vibrating on his well-rounded lips.

'*No yessss?*' his Dad asks, amused.

'I mean you can sleep after you've made a sizzling cup of coffee for me...'

'Sure-sure but...'

'No worry Dad. Tomorrow's a holiday so I'll surely make up for the lost sleep. These are the most crucial days...to decide things, right?'

'Right! Keep the spirit high!' the father gleams with satisfaction.

'Is Mom asleep? She couldn't take a nap in the day time due to pain.'

'Yes. I've given her the painkiller now. Do you suggest we hire some domestic help for a few days? You know...it is essential I think since you too are busy and I'm out the whole day...'

'Don't worry Dad. I'll manage.'

'But you need to...'

'I'll manage. Believe me I would. The operation has already cost us much plus the medicines for months...we'll have to tighten our belts.' Vyom pats his Dad's hand his eyes conveying more than tongue. Both the father and the son have in fact been proud of their minimalism.

Samarth, Vyom's Dad, is an official in PWD, an elderly gentleman who has saved penny after penny throughout his working period. He shudders to imagine how things could be managed if he had not. Sudha, his devoted wife has narrowly escaped death in an accident. Her entire jaw has been badly damaged and operated upon plus a few fractures in other limbs as well.

He is making coffee for Vyom, his mind all alert in-case Sudha needs some help. He loves her too much indeed to imagine a life after her.

'Here we are! Coffee son.'

'Thanks Dad.'

'You're worth it!' Dad flashes Vyom an encouraging smile.

...

It is too hot in the little study room of his.

Never mind.

He strides up and down to work up a little breeze finally standing by the window gazing at the moon.

The moon has been a witness to the number of nights he's been working hard for.

The moonlight silver edges through the window, illuminating the room, its belongings and his dreams.

A peace gift from God.

He knows there is a beautiful world outside this room which would welcome him for sure once he has done the necessary preparation to face it eye to eye.

He is chasing his dream in all earnestness.

He has heard many a 'rags-to- riches' kind of stories and somehow he is assured within that he too...is going to write one.

Perched on the windowsill, Vyom watches sheets of rain at-once blotting out the world.

The commotion around is deafening.

Gashes of lightening are tearing open the sky.

Who would listen to his voice in the marketplace called life?

These and many more questions gnaw his insides often.

Hours tickle by and he doesn't get enough shut eye.

Presently he rises from the bed again, switches on the night lamp and starts reading a letter, perhaps a thousandth time.

...

'Dear Vyom,

It's my very first letter to you...to any guy in this life. I dunno how to. I've often noticed that 'smth' in your eyes which perhaps goes arnd by the name of 'love' or y wud u always come out of the blue as if whenever I'm in some trouble? How when I'm caught gossiping under breath and made to stand up, it's your finger which tells me at once where were we reading? How do you know I've forgotten my tiffin home and...I find yours at my bench? How do you silently place a safety pin on my bench when I stand in need of it? You've been taking care of me like a loyal friend...a silent friend though. I can't however remain mute any longer for I'm overwhelmed u know...and must name this caring and sharing. Well, I'm sure it would be very difficult for you to express your emotions since u r an introvert and an ambitious kind ...so here I go with mine...I know I may not be the right choice for your kind of a guy...I know I'm not that '*karwa chauth*' kind of ritualistic gal who'd serve your parents with the same devotion as you do. Till date I have been a carefree girl... you know...living for the moment and letting the wind take me where it will...but I...I think I'm changing you know! And I don't want this relationship to stand on 'jus' frens' footing because if I do, I would be lying...u know. I know I'm a little eccentric kind but then...it sounds weird...but how dull would life be if there was no chirrup in life errr...or mood swings u know? U know what my friends say? They say you r a *khadoos...khadoos* you know! Plz... plz...plz...change a bit...for my sake? I k.n.o.w. there's no place for love in your life unless you achieve your goals and kind of big talk u know... but I'm kind of over-head and heels in love with you. If this sounds a little weird, it's all right. I don't care. I...I am nothing but a sickly plant that keeps sulking unless you cast it a look...and...and it perks up at once if you do! What do you call it? I choose to call it LOVE. Stop caring for me if you don't love...

Can't say 'forever yours' or smthn like that until you choose to...'

...

Vyom smiles a sour smile.

He loves Tia more than anyone else but...he can't admit the fact. He'd be distracted. He therefore pretends that he doesn't care. It pains him a lot...a lot indeed. He's seen many people hooking up. Not jus' hooking up but getting out of control. They don't even realize that 'a love thing' is needed between two people before they have sex. Word gets around quickly in schools and colleges as who is dating who. He believes that the longer a teenager says no to sex, the more time he is giving his brain to catch up with the hormonal changes his body is undergoing at the time.

...

Tia however had made up her mind to move ahead but had desperately tried to meet him one last time before she left the town for hostel life.

He didn't see her.

If he did, the fever of passion kept at bay for so long, might override him.

He very much wanted to have her in his arms because he knew he would be so lonely...so very lonely...without her crooning around.

The pain of impending separation and deep love never expressed, smothered him.

Most of his friends had moved to Kota back then.

Tia too.

He wasn't sure however.

His parents needed him.

He couldn't desert them.

...

Brooding over the choice of career and the preparation thereof, Vyom dozes off...

*****

11

Rohan 'n' his Angels

Hi Diary

Can't hold any more! I've gone through much during the whole year you know. You might be thinking *ki* where I was...why not sharing anything with you for so long. Actually I didn't realize how the entire year slipped by!

'*Hanji jaisa aap kahen...*' I had replied when Mom-n-Dad had told me *ki* '*Kota bhejne ka plan hai tujhe...*'

The moment I touch the bubble of past, the scene conjures up live as though!

...

We were in car-me and Mom-Dad returning from my Board Exam Centre. It was my last exam of the Tenth Board I had been toying with the idea that I would celebrate with my friends as I reached home but the eloquent outpouring of my parents vis-à-vis my future made me shudder.

I felt like running somewhere very far.

I didn't want to leave my gang behind.

I loved my buddies.

I loved my 'babe' too.

I loved the hang out places that the small town provided.

I loved my school, basketball court...

I jus' l.o.v.e.d. e.v.e.r.y.t.h.i.n.g...*yaar!*

The dream of being a doctor was not my parents' alone; it was my dream too...but...why leaving *my girl* behind *yaar?*

There were frequent talks at home and the weather got stormy-n-then stormier with each passing day...eventually they won.

I lost.

The form was filled.

I was sent to Kota.

Leaving the family was kind of welcome for you wouldn't have to listen to their no stop lectures-n-all but leaving Aliya, my girl behind melted me through and through.

I cried.

And then I cried lot more.

From the day one in Kota, I had been phoning her.

She didn't jus' pick up for a few days.

I thought *ki chalta hai, naraj hogi mujhse...mana lunga*...jus' one *Temptation,* a greeting card and a full passionate kiss would heal the wound whenever we met next.

My heart would drop every time my phone lighted up with a text, u know, I knew I was crushing HARD.

I-liked-her-so-much-I-couldn't-breathe.

But I was appalled to know that she had changed her number.

I was worried.

Obviously.

The worst however was still to come.

I came to know through a common friend that she had patched up with Sahil, one of my friends.

Good friends as such!

It was so rude, no?

Arrey at least we could have had a sober break-up before she patched up afresh...no?

An average student, I couldn't really cope-up with the rigorous classroom sessions that obviously culminated into serious health hazards with me.

Dream city.

They say they sculpt better human beings there. Many like me come to Kota with dreams to become doctors and engineers. Most of them dream of cracking AIPMT or IITs but eventually some have to return in despair.

I mean things turn sour with time.

We were forced to follow a rigorous routine of studying 15-16 hours a day with a high intake of junk food you know. Sleeping for a few hours and that too with the help of sleeping pills was really taking a toll on my health. I had been carrying tablets in my bag. I took them when fatigue seemed to have the better of me. Couldn't enjoy any meal as they mostly comprised of xtra oily *chole-bhature, pao-bhaji* etc.

I somehow survived.

The number of suicides among students left us all vulnerable.

I missed Mom-Dad.

I missed my childhood when there were no worries.

I missed my girl.

Naturally...I screwed up with my assignments and burying my face in the pillow, cried my heart out. I hid my face against my knees and jus' let everything flow...I switched on the AC and standing an inch close to it, let out a glass shattering shriek as if some-one had jus' breathed his last.

Know what? Sahil was my very first friend in the school. We would share everything- our tiffin, our dirty secrets, our school bunks, our wildest fancies and much more...and he knew pretty well who was my first crush ever...

...even then she ditched me and he betrayed my faith!

I hate friends!

...

Have you ever been in a foul mood?

Perhaps I gave it some 'drama' by slamming my door or maybe I was so angry that I slugged the wall with my fists jus' to emphasise that I was mad.

Days passed.

I tried to put up with the classes but miserably failed. We had tests usually on Sundays. It was my very first test and I ended up attempting only a few questions. The bell rang like a cruel reminder that I was a failure...

We were given the answer keys...

I scored in –ve.

Allen prayer, Allen Pratigya, doubt sessions, discussion classes, weekly tests, monthly tests ...I was sick!

The strict competitive environment sucked.

You had no other option than be what you were there for.

I was depressed like hell...made rude cuts on my hands...did no dressing and slept with the damn pillow over my face.

I slept till noon the next day, my eyes were damn swollen.

I sensed that a killing headache was all I was in for.

Someone banged the door.

A sudden fear snatched at my heart.

Could it be Dad?

O God please *nahin!*

My fingers quivered in apprehension.

Aah! It was one of my new friends, Sunny.

A good boy with lots of bad habits.

He was laborious, u know, had got rank under 500. He was dying of excitement and wouldn't mind throwing a gala party on the occasion.

'What's this?' he noticed my cuts and felt sudden abhorrence seeing them congealed.

He slapped me hard!

Huge sobs and sighs shook me.

'Ladki ke peeche kat le saale khud ko! Tere baap ne isiliye paida kiya hai naa tujhe? Bloody...' he let out a blood curdling scream.

Don't plz take notice dear diary. Abuses were freely hurled amongst buddies. They were like...like...helping verbs you know...kind of...☺

'Chal ab dressing ki to jaroorat nahin bachi. Chal kuch thoosne chalet hein. Tere iss bhai ka exam maal hua hai. T- shirt daal, Patolle vekhne chal!' commanded my Punjabi buddy yanking at a T- shirt the edge of which was peeping out of my wardrobe.

The entire bunch of clothes tumbled out of the wardrobe and he collapsed amidst those.

'Damn!'

While walking through the long corridor I told him everything since the very first chapter of my love story including my current low score.

'Arrey appan hi saale sab kuch pad lenge toh toppers kya karenge... leddem study dude...tu to chill maar.'

We went to the mess, wolfed down *daal-chawal,* stared many girls, giggled, chatted and commented upon their silky hair and silkier legs.

I came back to my room.

I still missed *my girl.*

I stared long at the photograph of my Mom-Dad that was propped up on my study table.

I missed Mom.

Wished she were there right then!

I would've clasped to her and...she would've wiped my pains away.

I regret that I've lived my life in such a way that my mother loves me more than anything, and yet doesn't like me at all.

I regret that I'm not what you wanted Mom.

You always ask why I can't finish things I do, and it's because I jus' want to find the one thing I can do to make you proud, Mom.

...

Why did we grow up *yaar!*

...

I missed my morning lectures for I slept till late.

...

The sound sleep had recharged my batteries.

It was not certainly the end of the world.☺

I activated my FB account which I had deactivated before coming to Kota. I started searching my new and old friends...gals actually...messaged to many, sent friend requests and waited with abated breath.

None accepted. ☹

Sunny taunted-'*Koi na puttar, haar ni mante...laga rah...*'

I laughed. We laughed. We laughed like mad! After so many days!

And it was again after so many days the next morning I attended my classes full flashed.

Ekchualllly I had reached the class a little earlier.

Jaake second last row mein centre mein tik gaya.

Next came two chics.

One was a 'beauty' and the other was 'yuck!'

Sunny came in like *kabab mein haddi* but he didn't prove so. He poked the soft flesh of my upper arm and nudged-'*maal hai maaal, ja pata le.*'

'*Yr kya kahun?*'

'*Naam hi puch le!*'

I went close to her, was about to ask her name but then my eyes caught sight of her identity card. So, she was Sarah. I came back like a *phussss patakha*, smiling a fake smile to her.

She smiled too!

She looked intrigued in-spite of herself; shot me a naughty glance and...one more smile...!!!

Well...now I could live without...☺

...

What was her name dude? ;)

We were allowed to carry mobiles to the classes. My *kameena dimaag* came in form. I opened my FB account, searched her name and found her in jus' one go.

I sent her a friend request along with a passionate message which was but obviously accepted.

...

We started chatting.

We'd sit in the last row to escape notice and so many paper chits were exchanged.

...

Finally we met.

I confessed what I'd recently gone through...how I'd come to Kota and all...how Aliya had broken my heart and spat me out...

I found her eyes red rimmed.

Our personal mobile numbers were exchanged...

She also came out with honesty...told me that she liked me at the very first sight...sixth sense...you know...kind of...that tells you that...'that's the one!'

Her caressing touch and velvet voice made my stomach...umm...quiver within.

'I...I think I love you Sarah.'

Maine jaldi hi bol dala.

Internet age!

It would be such a criminal waste of time otherwise!

No time to wait!

'Well, I think I feel the same.' she admitted too.

Phir kya tha?

We kissed.

Sarah was dressing my internal wounds.

We would jus' hang around; go shopping, movies, dhabas -n-restaurants. We'd go romantic at odd places and kiss oblivious of our surroundings.

Life was beautiful once again. ☺

This went on for the entire year.

I forgot everything but for my new girl.

And yeah...studies were gone too.

Winter was close. Mom was inviting me home and I like a stupid donkey was giving lame excuses. She wanted me to take my woollens to Kota but I cared not. Who wore hand knitted sweaters these days?

...

One night, probably in March, as were talking on phone, Sarah suddenly got sentimental and said things which I always scampered from.

FUTURE.

The word terrified me for...I knew...perhaps I had no bright future ahead.

'Babe I want to spend life beautifully with you. *Uske liye sabse jyada jaroori hai achhi job...aur uske liye jaroori hai achha college... aur uske liye...'*

I agreed.

We needed to study hard.

I couldn't sleep.

I couldn't afford to lose her.

I rang her up again past midnight and told her that I'd work hard.

...

Soon our eleventh class was officially over.

We were given a fortnight break.

I came back home and jus' roamed around.

'Is everything going on well son?' Dad asked one day.

'Absolutely yes dad!'

'We want a good result. That's what we sent you for, remember this.'

'Sure.' my heart did somersault within, absolutely overcome by an overabundance of parental advice.

...

As I went back to Kota, I found something missing.

Sarah was not the same.

She fussed over trifles and locked horns with me over petty things.

'Why do you behave like a possessive lover? I hate restrictions, you understand? That's why I'm here in Kota, away from home. I hated to be confined within the four walls of my classy home where my parents were always busy in meetings or social gatherings and servants kept a watch over me...the *'babe'. 'Babe'* my foot! Like I was still a *baby!* Actually my parents had no time to notice that I had grown up and I needed someone to talk...to share...to love...to be loved by.' Sarah uttered between convulsive sobs.

'Shhhh! Is my *babe* that much hurt?'

I wished I could take the word back that she hated the most.

Babe.

I wanted her to be mine.

Jus' mine.

No FB *pey* chatting with other guys and no friendship...I mean male friends...

Actually I was afraid of losing her, you know.

She'd often shout at me. 'All my friends have boyfriends but none of them is mean like you. Yes that's what you are...m.e.a.n.!'

Days were changed.

We talked less; fought more.

I steeled myself for what was to come next.

I needed to find out the reason.

Sunny came to my help again.

Ekchulllly she had been double dating! She'd found another guy and perhaps was waiting for an official break-up on the day when I'd leave for my home town for the NCERT preparation.

She would often accuse me that I suspected her...now someone might go and ask her whether I was wrong if I did?

I didn't want to allow her to ditch me though unofficially she already had.

'*Kya chal raha hai?*' I shouted.

'What do you mean? And by the way who gave you the right to talk to me in this way?' she snapped.

'As if I *dunno* anything!' I made faces.

'Who cares?' a bemused smile on her beautiful face.

'Means you confess?'

'Get lost! I don't want to have a boyfriend who sounds like a husband, you know...actually I don't need either a boyfriend or a husband. I can live on my own.'

'Okay. Let's not behave like kids. Let's talk. Listen. Sit!' I grabbed her shoulders and sat her on a chair.

I lowered down my volume for we were in a restaurant.

'I really want to marry you babe! I mean...Sarah! Don't you?' I passionately asked playing with this *marriage-thing-card* that never failed with girls. That's what I had known till date.

'Oh c'mon! I *dunno* if I'll ever get married. My motto is never to hold on to anything. I accept...n...then let go. Or it'll get to my head.'

'Am I...getting to your head?' I could hardly believe this was the same girl who was never tired of loving me; who would kiss me randomly whenever she noticed a spark of desire in my eyes. No matter for how long you professed to have known a girl...there were layers and layers to her!

'I'm shocked Sarah! You said you were ready to spend your entire life with me and suddenly what happened during this brief interval...that...that you sound so aloof?'

'Waiter! Two Cokes please!' she smiled generously towards the waiter and then back to the sour expressions for my unworthy sake.

'Calm down. See, I am not the kind of girl who goes for funny concepts like *ghar basaana chahti hun* and types...I agree, we've had a picture perfect romance. See, I am not ready to settle with picture perfect love...a job, a husband, a house, a dog, a car and kids...the standard dreams of any standard girl.'

'Tum chahti kya ho?'

'I want adventure, uncertainty and thrill. I am an independent girl who doesn't take marriage as a necessity. There're thousands of marriages solemnized every day. What of that? I've never encountered a single marriage that might've made me want to buy into the institution.'

'We live on the same planet Sarah. I'll live to see the day when you finally get bored of this freedom mania and all. You might be surrounded by people and loved by friends outside home but you'll feel so utterly alone when home. You'll need one person to belong to; will crave for the one who belonged to you...' I was almost at the verge of tears.

'Look, I need my own time and my own space. I'm far too practical to go crazy for romantic notions like be in need of *someone special to grow old with*...I have an education and I can make my own money. Love comes last on my list. *Aur vaise bhi* one can happily trade sex for the comfort of having someone by your side on the couch...*rahne bhi de tu nahin samjhega*...you are a typical *desi* kind of a guy I can't live my whole life with. We just don't fit well together. I hope I've made myself clear.' she rudely concluded.

'These itchy feet will lead you nowhere I tell you *Babu! Tumhe laut ke meri bahon mein aana hi padega.'* I did feel we were two jigsaw pieces from two different puzzles, a complete mismatch.

'Now that's what I strongly dislike about you! I hate guys that are sentimental.' She enjoyed each sip of Coke. Her shapely lips painted burgundy, left marks on the straw she was using.

'Fine. I am sentimental. But may I know your future plans?'

'You know very well that I'm a travel enthusiast. I'm already fed up of lectures on discipline by my parents and I feel travelling alone is the panacea I need.'

'Don't you think the very thought is daunting enough...I mean a girl dreaming to travel all alone to far off places? Are you not afraid of...a.n.y.t.h.i.n.g.?'

'I need to fight my fears. I need to take a break from my friends, my family, you and Sahil etc.etc. I prefer to choose my kind of happiness. You live only once you know...'she gave a wry smile as if not sure of what she said.

'So...?' I avoided my voice go emotional again yet made gestures inadvertently that reflected my anxiety, my restlessness, and my pain.

'So...if you want...one last time...' she stood up and opened her arms for a hug.

I looked away.

'Stop biting your nails for God's sake!' she came closer to where I stood like a fool calculating my losses.

She had to bend a little to reach my lips for she was wearing those high heels I had bought her a month ago. *Vaise bhi meri height to tumhe pata hi hai...kuch khas nahin hai...*

We kissed full.

'Sarah please!' I grabbed her hand.

'No ways! Let's pack our bags and move on.' she freed her hand, smiling.

She packed her desires, the so-called picture perfect love and walked away...to unpack somewhere else may be.

I stood on the same spot for long, feeling lost.

I came back to my room, took my clothes off, and went to the washroom.

I turned the tap on.

I didn't want to hear myself crying for a girl again.

...

...

You know how it is these days...

I wake up early and have six tuitions a day.

Six! Mind it!

I keep myself busy the whole day.

I miss *mi-angels*.

I'm sure they miss me too.

But who knows the working of a gal's mind!

Tell you what? When I returned home, I'd often fall asleep with little hiccupping sighs and sobs. My fingers would hover over the digits of her contact number unable to decide if I should. I'd then blink back my sudden *stttupid* tears and soon begin with a fresh bout of them.

...

One night I gathered the courage to ask her why after all did she do what she did to me.

It was her Mum who received my call.

'Listen Rohan. Sarah doesn't want to talk to you. Concentrate on your studies. This is the most crucial year to decide your future... blah blah blah...'

FUTURE!!!

Let's not talk too big...

...

Shhh!!!

...

...

I have found *a new babe*...

Not actually a girl *yaar!*

It is...

It is...jus' fantastic you know!

HER name is *Ecstasy*.

I first took it in capsule mode when I was at a dance party cooling around with guys-n-gals. You know what? I denied at first but then propped up by *frens*, I had it. It was tremendous man! I lost my perception of time and surroundings, my energy level rose to crack open as if; sort of euphoria you know...a little to be taken orally and then h.e.a.v.e.n. At another rave party, I saw a guy who'd stuffed himself with Ecstasy, repeat for hours: 'I'm a banana, don't peel *meee*, I'm a banana, don't peel *meee*.' Another fancied he was a butterfly and wouldn't stop hitting against the window!

...

...

To admit dear...

I suffer from extreme drug craving these days. I have been suffering from loss of hair. I'm getting very moody, can't concentrate during the classes, am sleepless most of the times and have low appetite. When I sleep, am startled in between, and find my teeth grinding...*dunno* what's happening...I have panic attacks...my face is blotched. There're bags under my eyes.

Parents keep nagging you by asking their favourite fall-back questions about your studies, your ambition and on and on and on.

I really don't have the heart to toss off flippant, outrageous responses to them so...

...I remain quiet.

They glance over to gauge my response.

I...don't talk to parents much.

What's the use...?

*****

12

Lemme Fly Highhh!!!

Scene one-

Trisha wears a pair of light blue shorts she has carefully torn. She has even recently learnt some embroidery designs and especially tried them on her shorts. It took her an entire day to make the pattern which is- 'a few flying birds and the words *'Lemme Fly Highhh'*. She takes a full view of her trim beautiful form in the mirror. Her top slips off her shoulders every second and that's how she likes it. It's a cute red top that perfectly goes with her trendy nail paint.

She's recently been experimenting with the make-up stuff a lot. Her Mom like usual, has banned it officially not knowing that if she bans it, it will only make kohl look more attractive to her teenage heart.

'I hate to see you plastered in foundation! And what posture is this for God's sake? It'll lead to back and neck pain in later life, do you understand?'

'*Later life?* Like what's that? Trisha asks supressing her grin.

'Your body language speaks a lot. If you maintain correct posture and stand tall and confident, people know you are a relaxed person. They immediately know what you want in life.'

Ragini maintains her composure showing she is relaxed too.

May be by this, her daughter knows what Mommy wants.

...

Scene two-

'For God's sake Mum! Stop stuffing me with these stuffed *paranthas* of yours! *Gimme* some sprouts rather.'

'Ho-hai! And all this sacrifice for...?' Ragini gives a snort of laughter.

'As if you don't know! *Khud bhi to dieting kar rahi ho naa?* Well, I'm doing the same for the same purpose.' sings Trisha.

'Well, that puts me in my place.' Ragini confesses with a smile.

'My waist is 29 inches presently which I have to bring to 28 in jus' one month you know or how will I go for my low waist *lahanga?*' Trisha sniffs with a pretended air of displeasure pinching at the flab of her Mom's waist.

'It's our Silver jubilee of marriage, not yours honey!'

'So what? Don't I have to look beautiful too?'

'Of course- of course!' Mom teases the daughter pinching her waist too.

'Ouch *Maa!*'

'The dance teacher may be here any moment. Will you dance with these hair rollers in your hair?' asks Ragini.

'I'm gonna *WhatsApp* Nikki. We'll learn the dance steps together or we won't be able to harmonise later.'

'Fine fine! Even I have to get the dinner prepared before he comes.' says the mother with a toss of her pony tail.

Trisha is presently very excited.

She takes out her knick-knacks from the drawer and examines them closely giving a final thought which one would go with her party dress the best. Unable to decide, she keeps them all on the bed to have an expert opinion from Nikki.

Nikki arrives dressed in a short sky-blue frock. She wears tiny ear hoops that dance with excitement as she gives a warm hug to Trisha.

'Looking fab yaar! When did you get this frock stitched? Keeping secrets *haan?*'

'*Arrey nahin!* My aunt brought it from Singapore.' Nikki smiles ear to ear.

'Whatever! Its lovely *yaar!* I'll borrow it someday when...' she takes a pause which is at once depressing.

'When?' Nikki's brows dance with mischief.

'No dates presently! Mom says.'

'And you are such an obedient and a nice girl!' winks Nikki.

'Who cares to be?'

'What about Ronny?'

'Ronny what?'

'I mean, I heard he apologised and all?'

'He did. He even sent me a few gifts after the incident promising to be loyal and all...' her pulse quickens.

'Hmmm?'

'Nothing yaar! I need a break...though...'

'And what before that...?'

'Jus' one last meeting with him to savour...until I find someone else...' Trisha winks. Dimples flash on her cheeks with a fresh glow anticipating a meeting with the lady-killer.

'Yeah! You may definitely borrow this dress for the occasion. Hee-hee.'

'*Vaise* why don't you too choose someone?' asks Trisha.

'Well...how about the dance teacher?' her eyes skitter away to rest at the doorway.

'Shut *uppp!* He's...'

'Gay...?'

'No! OMG! He's *marrrrieeeed!*'

'So what?'

'?????'

'So what darling? It's rather welcome no?' exclaims Nikki.

'!!!!!'

'YESSSS! They're more experienced you know…'

'YOU ARE A…!' compliments Trisha with teeth clenched.

'*Ahaaan*! And who you are?'

'What do you mean?'

'I mean you must know that I know everything wicked going on in your w.i.c.k.e.d. mind.' giggles Nikki.

'I *dunno* what you're talking about.'

'*Ahaan!* The way he puts a proprietorial arm around you to make you comfortable with certain dance steps…the way he pulls you with a sharp tug and you are all mad…with desire.'

'Shhh! He does the same to you, no?'

'No he doesn't! Frankly speaking I start melting even if it's the tip of his finger touching my forearm…but he has gone *lattooo* on you!'

'My God Nikki! You are too much! Do I ever feel green-eyed when the tuition sir gestures you to occupy the chair next to his? I can hear his stupid heart beat when his hand touches you by chance. By Chance? No! The way he explains things digging into your eyes or when his hand touches your straps…or…'

'Shut *uppp!* He's…'

'Gay…?'

'No! OMG! He's *marrrrieeeed*!' Both shoot a mischievous glance at each other, a gaggle of gossips and giggles, spreading their negligible bulk over a flowery silken sofa.

'You know what?' Trisha draws a long, heartfelt breath.

'Yes I do!'

'*Whaaat?*'

'I know that your crazy heart longs for such close proximities...I know you want someone...anyone...to draw you close...and...tighten his arms around you...'

'You are wicked!' her cheeks are flaming.

'I know I'm!' chortles Nikki.

The doorbell rings.

They spring from the bed.

'Must be him!' Trisha's voice is lazily pleasant.

*****

13

The Paper Dreams

Rohan had soon got over his love fever for Aliya and is reported to be in dole drums afresh on account of his recent breakup with Sarah.

Aliya's been home for a month not keeping well. She doesn't talk much to her parents nor calls on her friends as she normally would. She feels she has ceased to be the centre of attraction.

None bothers about her.

At least that's what she feels.

Sahil, her boyfriend after Rohan, has recently died in an accident. Died indeed. He drank much and drove. And it was she who he was dropping home that night when the mishap occurred! She was traumatized for the moment, got him admitted to a hospital with the help of some passers-by.

She witnessed him succumb to his injuries that were fatal.

He was beyond the reach of all apologies now.

...

The police interrogation and the like...has been too heavy a stress upon her to handle. All alone.

Distress is written large on her face.

She feels lonely; longs for human company.

Two big tears of reminiscence drop down her eyes as she fabricates in her mind the lovely scenes of her childhood when all went jus' so smooth...

Her dad was not that successful a business magnate back then...

Her Mum waited anxiously for her to return from school and the two would share the day's happenings at length. Some real nice food would be waiting on the dining table and...how the two would eat and laugh and be really-really happy!

The Sunday outings and the home like feel...the chirrups...

...

The house however acquired grey shades and she grew up to be a wilful girl who apparently cared for none and who, none cared for. Her Mum was often in tears for her Dad hardly stayed home. It was always his parties, business meetings, club or his friends with whom he spent pretty good time and drank daily as a ritual.

Her Mom too eventually grew more and more neglectful to her daughter's needs as a teenager and got more and more indulgent towards her own.

She'd be out of doors for hours and hours at a stretch. Her heart chased something. But what? She knew not.

...

Aliya is nostalgic.

She tries to push her beautiful past into oblivion.

...

She looks at the door with no hope of her parents' return presently.

She sits on the cold floor.

Her throat feels parched.

Her heart too is parched somewhere at the root.

...

It's 4 AM.

Her mother can be heard climbing the stairs to her bedroom.

Aliya follows her, unnoticed.

Mom is humming. She throws her footwear away having some difficulty to maintain balance while she does. Seemingly she is drunk. She enters the room and has a look in the giant mirror by the bed. She can discern the slight aging lines around her eyes, decides to overlook them and begins humming again.

She is in the grip of hangover. She slips into a satin nighty and throws her drowsy self on the bed muttering something.

Aliya tries to listen absorbedly; unnoticed still.

'Oh! Thanks to the parties like this. Ummm...at-least some nights you can feel all fresh and new again sleeping with a blind date and reaching those levels of gratification where your daily partner can't dream of taking you. Thank God! My keys matched with the one for whom my heart always fluttered. What if it was *my* husband? Oh No! God can't be that unfair.' she thinks aloud and laughs.

'Mom, I need to talk.' Aliya's impatience has the better of hers.

'*Haan?* Aliya! You woke up so early?' she looks cautious.

'I didn't sleep.' Aliya's voice trails off.

'Even I didn't. That's why I need to.' smiles her mother and gets into covers giving a drowsy grunt.

...

...

It's noon time.

Aliya stands in her mother's bedroom again.

Her mother stands before the giant mirror again.

The fragrance of perfume is everywhere in the room.

The mother greets her with an apologetic smile.

'Aliya, when do you have to go back to your hostel? It's been more than a month you're home. Must be getting bored, no? You can't while away your life if one of your friends has died. It happens...you know...that's how life goes...one must move on...'

her mother says in a matter of fact way while straightening her hair.

'For your kind information Mom, I have dropped studies.'

'Dropped what? What do you mean by that?' she switches the machine off abruptly still holding a lock of her hair in hand.

'I always mean what I say.'

'But how could you decide that and...and you bothered not to take my opinion or your Dad's?'

'Are you guys e.v.e.r. home?' Aliya's eyes bubble up.

'Am I not standing before you r.i.g.h.t. n.o.w. a.t. h.o.m.e.?'

'Yes you are! You came home at four early morning having spent the whole night out ... and now may be getting ready for your next party or whatever...Mom, do you ever bother to ask-'Aliya, my child, how are you?'

'How dare you talk to me like this? What else am I supposed to do? Keep waiting for you and Dad a.l.w.a.y.s.? Do I have no right to be happy?' her mother snarls, gripping Aliya's forearm.

'Leave me!' growls Aliya.

'Let your Dad come home. I'll...' the mother lets go her hand in anger.

'He'll come only when you are gone. That's the way it has been.' explains Aliya with dispassion.

'OMG! I never knew you had become so blatant!' the mother bites her lips, standing frozen in disbelief.

'You know nothing about your daughter except for the bitter fact that you have one.' Aliya retorts.

Slap!!!

'Even you need to remember that I am your mother! Mind it!' screams the mother.

Aliya's eyes seethe with resentment and pain.

She gives a wounded look to her mother and dashes for the staircase.

Her life seems to have been torn apart.

...

...

She wanted to discuss certain things with her Mom and Dad like...how shocked and pained she was after the accident... how guilty she had been feeling because it was she who had challenged Sahil if he could surpass the speed of other bikes their friends rode...how...above all, the niggling questions asked by the police been stressing her to death...!

She wanted to discuss her future plans with her mother...that... that she didn't want to study further...that she wanted to be a model...that she'd already submitted her portfolio of pictures to some modelling agency...that she'd be leaving for Gurgaon soon.

What she craved for was a parting hug from her parents.

...

'Never mind!' she wipes her tears.

'I'm a grown up now. I don't stand in need of parental hugs and kisses. I'm a fledgling who had to leave home some-day to learn to fly.

Thisss the day.

...

Later...

'Hullo! Payal I'm coming to stay with you. You said you had a few contacts no...? Hmm...*chalo* bye!' Aliya sends a voicemail.

She's thrown in a few dresses of hers, a couple of warm clothes and other accessories.

She next peeps into her parents' bed room.

Her mother is not home.

Her Dad is seen curled up in the warm blanket, snoring.

She takes extra caution to escape notice and enters the room.

She can't help bestowing a kiss on her Dad's forehead.

She purses her lips to keep them from trembling.

Finding the keys at an easy approach, she slides opens the wardrobe carefully, so it would not squeak and takes out the desired amount plus a few gold ornaments.

'Plz plz plz God! Forgive me. I need to stand. And I need to survive. Hope you understand?' she mumbles looking ruefully at the little silver idol of Lord *Ganesha* in the wardrobe.

At the last moment, with the taxi hoking downstairs, she snatches up guiltily the couple photograph of her Mom and Dad from the showcase in the drawing room.

...

Aliya knows that modelling as a career can offer lucrative work and glamorous settings but she also knows that the industry is notoriously tough to break into.

Stiff competition, long working hours and big, impersonal casting calls are some of the less glitzy aspects of this industry.

If she has to give it a try, she has to learn how to take rejections without getting personal and *still be focussed*.

The modelling industry can offer great opportunities for money and travel, but it is not without risks. Illegitimate agencies or photographers, pressure to maintain a certain look or weight, and access to alcohol or drugs are some of the challenges teen models may run into.

You'll need a lot more than jus' a pretty face if you have designs on becoming a model.

Although some people are fortunate enough to be plucked out of shopping mall crowds by talent scouts, most aspiring models need to work hard to get themselves noticed by agencies and clients.

Making it in the fashion world will be jus' as much about your personality and work ethic as your appearance.

The role of understanding parents is quite crucial while launching a teen modelling career. Even signing with a modelling agency is not going to be a cake walk she knows for she doesn't carry parental approval which is required here.

Had her parents been supportive, things could have been pretty easy.

'I'll manage.' she still resolves within, shutting out the truculent voices inside her head telling her she shouldn't.

*****

14

AIPMT *Preps on the go!*

Exams are round the corner. Anushka is working hard. Her parents are working in alternate shifts so that one of the two remains home in case she needs their support.

'You haven't still finished your juice! What is this dear?'

'Oops! I'm so sorry Dad! I jus' forgot!' Anushka downs the juice in one go.

'That's like a good girl!'

'I'm done with my entire syllabus. Don't please bother. You may go and attend your patients.'

'You sure darling?'

'Pretty sure Daddy!'

'And the assignments?'

'I'm done with them as well.'

'You know what sweetheart? We are proud of you! Rank or no rank...your comprehension of things must be complete. We don't want to measure your qualification on the scales of percentage and marks. We want you to be independent and innovative.'

'Yeah Dad! I used to be pressurized by the thought what if someone else got the first rank which I'd got beautifully habituated to? But then...this grading system, you know...it really put us at ease. I do aspire to top but I'm out of that cut throat mentality to reach there now.'

'That should be the attitude darling.'

'Your Mumma was suggesting if we should go for some career-counselling thing. Do you think we should?'

'No Dad! Actually I have been surfing through the information available online regarding the career in medicine. I think we can manage, no?'

'Medical field contains a broad range of academic education other than MBBS. It contains the certified courses, medical diploma courses, bachelor degree courses, master degree course and many other short time knowledge booster courses for medical professionals. The candidates having PCB or PCMB group in their +2 can appear in AIPMT 2016 for admission to the top medical colleges in India.' Dad tells Anushka in the matter of fact way.

'Thank you my daddy the great! I need no career-counselling.' laughs Anushka.

'Daddy is always there darling. Do let us know in time if your area of interest lies somewhere else. What I mean is like if you aren't interested in the medicine line, you may go ahead with any other line of career. Say...modelling or acting...you know... you are so good looking...we have absolutely no objection to that.' laughs Daddy.

'So generous of you! I know I can do what I want. AND that gives me the extra boost to hitch my wagon to stars. Dad! I wonder what would I do without you. I mean how lucky I am to have such understanding parents like you!'

'It's an overwhelming sense of contentment.' her Dad's eyes well up.

'It's all the result of hard work you two have done for my sake Dad! Trust me I'll never let you down.'

'I do.'

'Thanks Dad.' Anushka radiates a beautiful smile.

'You may ring me for anything you want.'

'I know Dadda.' Anushka kisses her dad's hand.

*****

15

It's not jus' "A"

There are many...further down the Alphabet

Aliya has been desperate to get a chance in the fashion world. She leaves early morning with her portfolio and comes back around midnight, bone-weary and depressed. Apparently she is squandering her energies and money both.

Why is she putting herself through the torments?

She doesn't know.

It's almost a month she's been sharing the apartment with Payal.

Aliya presses the door-bell.

Payal responds a little later than expected.

Aliya feels guilty like she was an intruder into somebody's personal space.

She must not take friendship for granted.

What if Payal throws her out on the road?

She's been brooding hard entire nights.

A foul mood.

...

She is a little surprised by the sounds of laughter inside.

Payal slightly pushes a guy out of the living hall, clutching his shoulders.

The guy bumps into Aliya.

71

'Aa...ha...! So you are Aliya, right?'

'Well...I am Aliya. Right.'

'*Bande ko Prashant bulate hein*. Glad to meet you.' The guy offers a hand shake. His palms are slick with sweat.

'Yes! She is Aliya I told you about. No handshakes! Now you should leave.' reminds Payal.

'No parting kiss today?' he runs his fingers on his lips.

Aliya looks away in hesitancy.

'Come out you! Errr...Aliya you may go upstairs and change. I'll join you shortly.' Payal pulls him by his tie laughing.

Aliya climbs the stairs but then feels an urge to lean against the railing and watch audaciously.

The guy slightly pushes Payal to the garden wall, removes her small leather jacket and kisses her neckline madly. Payal looks aroused too. She grabs his hair with both hands and pulls him to place his thirsty lips upon hers. They kiss, smooch and breathe hard. Prashant seems aware of Aliya's presence around. He advances further and holds Payal still closer whispering something.

Aliya feels stimulated.

Next he pulls Payal to his car parked in the porch.

Aliya isn't sure if she's made a right choice to stay with Payal.

...

Aliya lies in bed.

So many things are running together in her head.

...

Each moment has been a stake through her heart.

A little later...

Payal's small jacket lies on a chair.

She's slipped into Tee and shorts.

'Did you have lunch?' asks Payal with concern.

'Lunch and dinner I care not for. I grab almost anything I come by. I jus' have to be a model.'

'Being a model is not a cakewalk you understand? Professional photographs are essential for beginning a career as a teen model. Look for professional photographers who specialize in headshots or fashion editorial. If professional photography services are too expensive, consider hiring a photography school student. Since students are building their photography portfolios, they will often agree to photograph you for free. Instruct the photographer to take both headshots and full body shots in various settings. Bring several outfits to the shoot, but keep things simple and natural looking. Agents want to get a sense of what you actually look like and how well you photograph.' enlightens Payal making her a drink of Vodka.

'Hey how do you know this much about modelling?'

'Contacts darling!' winks Payal.

'AND if you don't mind what contact was he?' Aliya laughs.

'Who? The guy? Obviously not my bro.' Payal giggles.

'What else do you know mmm...I need to know...to be a model?' asks Aliya with a made-up grave look.

'Hmm now you seem to be in receptive mood. Well, standards are high in the fashion world, and competition is fierce. You'll need to be dedicated to keeping yourself in shape and looking your best at all times if you're going to have a successful career as a model. It is important to eat well, exercise regularly and get plenty of sleep. Avoid foods and lifestyle choices, such as heavy alcohol consumption, that will have a negative effect on your looks and prevent you from staying focused on your career.'

'Wow *yaar!* I don't know whether I have made a right choice about my career but I'm sure of one thing.'

'And what's that?' Payal asks, intrigued.

'That I did the right thing coming to you.' beams Aliya.

'Well, no doubt about that.' laughs Payal.

'I'm sorry but I can't help asking errr...'

'Ask *naa!*'

'Were you guys in living-in or smthn? I mean I have seen him the first time. I have been here for the entire month! I guess I have disturbed your love life.'

'Chalta hai yaar.'

'???'

'I would've managed more but he's going to see his parents in Pune for a week or so. So, we decided to, you know, *gv sm* quality time to each other, hang-out together you know...jus' to enjoy.'

'What was going on in the car?' Aliya's insides twist as she asks inoffensively, knowing it's a wrong question though.

'Love-making, what else?' exclaims Payal, her mouth turned up derisively.

'I mean...'

'I know what you mean darling. *Thisss* is the right time babe! See; a girl fears male company as long as she has her virginity intact. Once that is gone, all fear gone. I mean nothing beyond that; right? AND by the way do you think you are going to become a model without such give and take?' Payal offers her the drink.

'Is this the only way a girl can move ahead in life...I mean if she is ambitious to reach the top?' she is confronting her own demons.

'It's a vast universe of fantasies honey AND *everything has a price.'*

The glasses clink together.

Aliya pretends that it's not her first time but Payal is wide-awake to see through the pretence.

'See; if you go the l.o.n.g. way you'll have become old before you can realize your dream. The only short cut...' Payal runs her fingers at the brim of the glass. Alcohol is entering her bloodstream.

'In that case...I'm okay with it. I mean, let's see.' Aliya is cupping her elbows to stop herself from fidgeting.

Both laugh a fake laughter and get into the covers.

Payal leans in closer and draws in a deep breath close to her neck.

'You've spoilt me in a month!' whispers Aliya.

'That's what you came here for!' Payal's dark and unfathomable eyes run over her.

'I came here to realize my dream.' Aliya murmurs.

...

'Asleep Aliya?' croons Payal after a couple of silent moments gone.

'Umm. Not yet.'

'Let's talk then.' says Payal.

'Why not?'

Both sit up reclining their elbows on pillows.

'I have some secrets.' says Payal in a sombre tone.

'Evrybdy has.'

'Let it go then if u are not interested.'

'Hey! Listen no, Payal?'

'Now what?'

'Say *naa;* what secret?'

'Hmmm...*toh*...u really wanna know?'

'Haan baba!'

'I was going remarkably well with my studies...' Payal begins straightaway.

'Go on. *M listenin.'*

'I heard the girls talking. My classmates. They commented upon my figure saying I wasn't good enough to attract a guy. The girls even talked about my negligible cup size and...grrrrr ...!'

'Aah but why the hell was it a business of theirs? I mean...'

'Right. So I was angry. Very angry. Who the hell were they to predict what I was going to get in my life? Bloody mean girls! I started suffering from worthlessness. I'd stand before the mirror for hours! And each time I did, I couldn't muzzle that inner critic that told me I was worthless.'

'To have good self-esteem, you have to like *urslf.'*

'I hated *myslf.* I had suicidal thoughts.'

'Aah! Then?'

'I ate more and more to put on some weight and get into a nice acceptable shape. You know how it is with girls. They have to be watchful about their hair, their nails, their outfits, their armpits, skin, complexion and what not...if they aren't, they're thrown into the category of being unattractive and uninviting. Their future is damned!' Payal's gestures convey her frustration.

'It's not like that darling! When anyone commented on your body type or said something humiliating, you should've defied by saying something like *'Mind your own body image!'* or *'Oh, get a grip!'* or *'Who made you the body police?'*

'I couldn't. I had these damn tough issues to work out and I guessed I couldn't. It was inheritance! How could I? And I started gaining weight BUT at wrong places.'

'So?'

'So I thought getting messed up would be better. I had seen the trick on TV. I started getting high on cough medicine. I kind of knew about it. I easily got it from our medicine cabinet and drank like---the whole bottle!'

'I guess even I've heard about the thing. How was the feel anyways?' asks Aliya, intrigued.

'It was like...like getting really-really drunk. The thing grew frequent. The chemist denied the medicine to me unless I carried some doctor's prescription.'

'So?'

'When you decide to kill yourself, no one can stop you. I got the stuff from one of my seniors. I had to pay a heavy price for it though.' Aliya is at the verge of tears.

'???'

'I was drinking a lot! I got introduced to Oxycotin and Morphin pills as well. I couldn't handle my studies. Seriously. My grades were badly going down. All my pals had good families you know. People cared for them. Their family came to the school to see them at games but nobody ever came to see me at games and nobody ever said, *'Hey Payal! Go ahead! Keep up the good play! I'm proud of you!'* she melts into sobs.

'How did you react?'

'I never heard an *'I love you'* and all. I was angry. Very angry. And I would punch the wall in anger. I felt like I was a throwaway... like...like garbage you know. I didn't simply matter.'

'Your parents knew nothing? I mean your taking those drugs and all? I mean didn't they notice your odd behaviour?'

'They did. They asked a lot of questions in-fact. I lied.'

'You lied?'

'I LIED. What else could I do? They'd freak out, throw me out of the house. They wouldn't simply understand. They don't know how it is to be a teenager. I didn't want to disappoint them *yaar!* AND I didn't want to be yelled at!'

'What alibi did you cook then?'

'I told them studies were getting harder than ever. I promised I would try to pull my grades back up. The hallucinogenic trips these drugs caused were the only get away from my troubles. I used them more than ever to get high.'

'OMG! You have been through all this? I don't believe this! Jus' because someone commented upon your figure...hard to understand you know.'

'You can say that...' says Payal, looking at her ripe bust and perfect waist.

'But...it isn't that important you know.'

'It is!' Payal still fumes about the humiliation.

'I *dunno*...I mean...'

'The guy who bought you the cough medicine and other drugs... did he blackmail you into sex or something like that?'

'He did. Not only him...his friends as well.'

'*Ishhhh!!!*'

'And...what did you do with the empty bottles?'

'Intelligent question. You know what? Alarms would sound if they ever found an empty bottle of beer in a teen's car but they wouldn't think twice seeing an empty cough syrup or used up packet of tablets.'

'So, how long have you been fooling around?'

'Long back. Now *toh* they have shut their doors on me.'

'They gave up so soon?'

'Oh no! We had seven-days-a-week- blow up sessions at home. We would shout, cry and frustrate each other. They set curfews. They put me in therapy and all.'

'Hmm?'

'Finally they gave up saying- 'Fine. Okay. This is your life. Have it your own way.'

'At least you should have tried, you know...to...'

'I had given up too because my parents had never taught me that life didn't always go to plan...I didn't know that there might be an occasional necessity for a plan B or C or even further down the alphabet.'

'Hmm.'

'If I didn't pass the exam or couldn't make a good team, they never told me that there were some back up ideas as well. I didn't know that life meant a series of choices...what I was made to understand was that it was jus' a matter of 'making it' or 'failing.'

'What after that?'

'They were seeing but not seeing from the day onwards. I couldn't see them crying day and night for my worthless sake. Mum suffered from the pangs of guilt that she couldn't catch my symptoms of going astray despite being a psychologist herself!'

'Poor she!'

'I pitied her too. Therefore I left home. I left home because finally after many bouts of crying I saw myself as perhaps God saw me. God said, *'I am all the love you are looking for! I am all the love you need!'* And I set out to chase my dream.'

'You don't miss them?'

'I miss them intensely! I dial their numbers, speak nothing...they know...silent communication...kind of.'Payal bursts into tears. A weight that had been pressing down on her chest for so long has finally been given vent.

Aliya can understand the pain well.

She offers a bear hug to her friend, her eyes glittering like broken glass.

Both travel through the maze of their respective past until sleep pulls them under.

*****

16

Will Rohan Find Himself?

It's a small room with two single beds. Close to the door there is a poster of *Blue Eyes* by Yo-Yo Honey Singh. A few books here and there, sexy bombs stuck on the dressing room's walls. A few cigarettes lie spilling out of the pack on the bed-side table and a few smashed in the ash-tray.

'Jus' the place!' exclaims Rohan, light-heartedly, his heart ballooning at the sight.

Rohan looks thinner than ever, his scruffy student beard replaced by a trim, responsible looking moustache- grown.

Anurag is Rohan's cousin who has picked him up from the Metro Station an hour ago.

*****

Rohan was in depression having got habituated to Ecstasy. He would talk none, look drunk even after a bath and meet none. He'd jus' sleep. His parents got worried naturally and tried to have animated talks with him.

The boy who looked so lucid and full of life was sinking in permanent gloom.

Despite his hard reluctance, they somehow persuaded him to undergo medical tests and were traumatised to know that their only son was addicted to some drug.

Watching a loved one slowly disintegrate is one of the most painful experiences imaginable. Especially for parents...they however knew that any drastic change in his life could trigger further depression so they somehow managed to remain cool, calm and collected.

They consulted a psychoanalyst for they knew waiting could be fatal.

They didn't want him to wake up in some hospital next.

'Look son! We wish you to succeed in life. We have certain dreams for you like all parents have for their children. But the most vital thing for us is to ensure that you live a long and healthy life. We won't discuss the reasons that might've led you to the self-destructive path...' his father had swallowed a lump of pain down his throat.

'Don't do this to us son. It would be downhill all the way...for us all...' the mother had sighed trying to subdue the pain in her chest.

'I understand Papa! I don't really know what's happening! Even I want to come out of this passivity, this autumn of despair! Believe me. I do!'

The scenes were getting catastrophically humiliating.

'Why then...did you slash your wrist last night?' his mother had burst into an uncontainable pain.

'Mom! I didn't want to! I r.e.a.l.l.y. *dunno* what led me to that! I can imagine how you might've been pained seeing me awash with blood...but...things were getting beyond control...I always felt another drink wouldn't hurt. But then...my mind began playing tricks you know kind of. I realized my life had begun crashing down around me and I realized things were really-really going out of control you know!' Rohan had hidden his face in her lap.

'Perhaps we were demanding too much.' said the father in a trance like state.

'Demanding too much? We never asked him to share any household responsibilities. We jus' wanted him to study and catch up with those who always made their parents proud!' the mother had grudged.

'That's where...that's where we were mistaken Savitri. Every child is different. We can't expect the same amount of labour from all. Perhaps our Rohan doesn't have that calibre or maybe he does exceptionally well in some other field?'

'?????'

'Any field that his heart goes for...'

*****

'Hi diary,

Not in the right frame of mind to write but how I feel smothered! Depression, anxiety, stress, re-occurring nightmares at night and very-very bad headaches are killing me bit by bit. I'm almost dead I feel at times. This drug is very fatal you know. I wonder how am I still alive. Coping with my nightmares is too hard to handle. I often wake up in the middle of night thanking God that it's jus' another nightmare!

I pray these nightmares fade away before I do.

Now I hear guys and gals talking of this drug, calling it fun, a harmless drug.

All I can think of it now is- *If they only knew.*'

The next morning...

'Let's send him to his cousin Anurag for a few days. May be he opens up to him...and then...we can think of a cure.'

'But what about his classes and coaching?' asked his Mom looking puzzled.

'*Life comes first.*' Rohan's Dad had given the decisive answer.

*****

'*Kuch bana yaar! Bhookh se mara ja raha hun!*' barks Rohan at Anurag who is presently living as a tenant with another boy from his home town.

The two have been good phone pals for long therefore moved past the language of formality.

'I can prepare nothing except Maggi. *Chalega?*' asks Anurag.

He's been living away from home for three years trying to find his feet.

'Do that *phataphat! Daudega!*'

A little later both clean up the dishes cracking jokes and sharing their scintillating experiences with girls.

'Don't tell me dude you are a virgin?' asks Anurag, the elder of the two.

'I'm!'

'I don't believe an eighteen year guy to be a virgin! C'mon man! *Kis mitti ka bana hai tu?*'

'What to do *yaar!* Lot of restrictions at home. You can't move around with girls and then if you do get a chance...of-course by chance, the girls have too much of *nakhras* over there.'

'I'll take you to an awesome place with my gang. We'll hang around and *n'joi* to the fullest. Jus' forget the small town girls and their *nakhras* man! Jus' forget the whole world. *Zindgi na milegi dobara*; right?'

'*Aish karne hi to aaya hun tere pass. Haan ye baat aur hai ki Papa ne mujhe tujhse guidance lene ke liye bheja tha.'* sniggers Rohan.

'That's what I'm doing, no?' laughs Anurag.

'Get ready fast! Get ready for the high energy session shaking your body to the high watt music and unwinding with drinks. Yo!!!'

'Know what? I'm damn excited!'

'But beware! T.h.e.r.e. a.r.e. n.o.c.t.u.r.n.a.l. a.n.i.m.a.l.s. t.h.a.t. m.a.y. a.t.t.a.c.k. y.o.u.!!!' Anurag assumes a scary look running a thumb along his jaw.

'M waiting to be...a.t.t.a.c.k.e.d.' whispers Rohan, wiping the kitchen slab with doubled energy.

'Don't waste your oomph...man!'

'Yeah, right!'

...

...

*****

17

The Spark Rekindled

The guard at the Disc entrance is a fussy man who surveys Rohan and Anurag from top to bottom, cracks a few dirty jokes and then finally lets them in as Anurag has shoved a five hundred rupee note in his fist. The guard winks and Anurag warmly responds.

It's a dingy place that swallows them instantly. The smoke machine is spewing smoke and colourful lights frisk around. It looks like it's all enveloped in an enthralling black with flashes of red, green and blue. The ear splitting music makes their young hearts throb wilder. The wine counters are added charm by the shaven guys and seducing girls that serve wine, smile and wink.

It's an unreal world with fake smiles and made up faces.

People throw tantrums and fidget when they walk on crowded roads; they bark and spit abuses at each other when caught in a traffic jam but here they don't seem to mind their shoulders jostling against each other.

It rather tantalizes them.

Anurag is stimulated beyond limit.

Rohan's eyes light up too with huge excitement.

...

'He is h.o.t.!' comments Payal as she nudges Aliya.

'Hey wait a minute!' Aliya stammers as she has a look in the direction.

Payal moves ahead without bothering whether Aliya follows or not.

'Hi! I'm Payal.' Payal glows with a beautiful smile.

'Anurag.' says Anurag.

'Nice shirt!'

'Thanks.'

'Looks like I have seen you somewhere?' smiles Payal who is intent to have some good time even in Prashant's absence.

'Good going *haan! Mujhe bhi kuch kuch aisa hi lagta hai'.*

'Dance?' Payal grabs the chance.

'Sure! Why not?' Anurag is not dumb enough to reject such tempting offers.

Soon the two are swinging in each other's arms.

And very soon they abandon themselves to a good no-bars-kissing-session.

Who says humanity suffers segregation? Here nobody minds coming close to strangers. No body wears class tags. They cast amorous glances, invite, are invited, clink their glasses, caress, indulge in lip-locks and have one night stands...no mutual obligations...jus' fun...

Rohan gets enticed by the colourful clouds of smoke spurting out of the flavoured hookahs that rise high towards the ceiling.

A few guys stand by the hookah counters and invite him.

They look intrigued for their sixth sense tells them who is a new bird here.

'Which flavour man?'

'I...I mean...what flavours?' he stumbles.

'*Try Sweet Red Mint or Watermelon*. Watermelon is awesome! Why not try Mango...? You will be breathing out the thunder man! Wow! It smells so fruity! Jus' look at the sugar grains stuck on the very lid!'

Rohan smiles...copies the guy inhaling a nose full.

He then slowly opens his mouth and lets out the curly smoke, a hazy screen of smoke hiding him.

'Ten *outtta* ten...for the powerfulness of the taste?' asks the bald masculine guy with a gold ring hanging oddly at the end of his eyebrow.

'Holy shit man! What the fuck is this? I mean, it's too screwing! It's... it's too MANGOWY!!!' Rohan exclaims.

'Hoooooo!!! In My World things revolve around me.' they hoot.

'Well I do give ten out of ten to the lovely ringlets of smoke. Balls to balls!' Rohan gleams and winces inhaling the thing once more.

He is kind of super surprised to see Aliya standing behind the foggy screen.

'Hi Rohan!'

'Man! Is this...? Is this really you? Aliya?' Rohan trails the words, twitching his arm to make sure that he wasn't hallucinating from loneliness.

'Very much the me! Very much the same you knew...*Ittt izzz* Aliya.' Aliya walks straight through the smoke and embraces him.

'Oh babe! My Aliya!' Rohan clasps her composing his face into benign forgiveness.

'So, you aren't that fresh a guy we thought you were?' whoops break out from the hookah guys.

The one time love-birds walk sideways.

'I don't still believe my eyes.' gasps Rohan.

'My eyes have been chasing you since you entered the Disc.'

'Ohh really?' Rohan mops his brows.

'How come? You are here?' gulps Rohan.

'We had to meet again. That's it.' she wraps her arms around him and whispers in his ear.

Rohan is stung by the memory of the days spent with her and how he had cried the entire nights when she'd hooked up with the other guy.

'Wait a minute! You dumped me right?' a sudden hatred snatches at his heart.

His yanks his arm away.

'I was a fool. I need you Rohan!' says Aliya, her voice all silky.

...

'I missed you so much!' no edges to his voice now.

'Me too.' her eyes bubble up.

They hug.

Rohan feels blissful to have got his babe back.

Aliya is misty-eyed with hope and happiness.

'I love you! I still love you, you know.' says Rohan in a husky voice, snaking a lock of her hair.

'Me too Rohan. *Meeee toooo*!'

His hands slide smoothly up her back beneath her black top.

Aliya accommodates to the wild current of passion find its way.

'Let's sit somewhere else.' whispers Aliya.

He walks her out of the crowd and sits her on a sofa in some secluded corner and sits on a tripod himself. She runs her fingers in his hair.

Rohan grabs her shoulders, his eyes feeding deep upon her beautiful face.

'Rohan please!' her tongue denies while her eyes plead for more.

'My lips are parched. Can I have a drink?' she asks passionately.

'Why not sweetheart?'

...

Payal is still dancing with Anurag.

She's been eyeing Aliya and the unknown guy all this while.

She shakes back her hair, smiling.

'Don't go babe pleeeez! Let's...' pleads Anurag, his lips nuzzling the back of her neck.

'Chill babes! I'll be back. We'll...' winks Payal tracing the outline of his face.

Anurag shoots her a made-up sour look.

She smiles a wicked smile.

...

'Excuse me.' Payal approaches Rohan and catches him red-handed mixing something in the drinks.

'Hi! I'm Payal. Aliya is staying with me. I guess you are...Rohan, right?'

'So I am! How do you...know my name?'

'I know everything.' she smiles a cunning smile.

'So...?' Rohan throws a probing glance.

'Plan kya hai???' Payal does the same.

'Well; if you allow and give company to my bro Anurag...we'd...' smiles Rohan.

Payal radiates with an appealing smile and a strong scent of female perfume.

*****

18

Finally...Trisha has a Thing to Share!

Trisha is finally struck by Cupid's bow.

At least she firmly believes she is.

On one hand she is developing a soft corner for Ronny in her heart and has agreed to a date with him on the farewell day which would be mmm...very soon; on the other she is carried off her feet by the dashing, smashing dance teacher Ameesh whose role in their life as her mother assumes was over after the wedding anniversary of hers.

Ameesh is an energetic, physically fit and a confident dance teacher who has a successful track record of improving a student's knowledge and understanding about contemporary dance. He holds recognized teaching qualifications, has experience of teaching all age groups and not only fully understands the needs of his students but also has the ability to quickly engage with them. He's taught in a number of private dance schools, colleges and adult education centres. He has experience of teaching ballet, tap, ballroom, jazz, hip-hop and contemporary dance.

His expertise at using movements, gestures and body language to portray dance routines has somehow triggered passion in Trisha's teenage heart. She's developed romantic feelings for him. During the private dance sessions for the family function she began dressing in increasingly suggestive clothes to the point that he felt uncomfortable holding her in a closed position in front of Nikki and a few of her friends. She would often linger after the lessons and continue holding his hand.

Unable to resist any longer even Ameesh seems to have begun developing the same kind of feelings for her.

She is a lovely girl in all respects.

He can no longer maintain clear, professional boundaries that are absolute.

It looks like he literally stands in the shoes of her idealized romantic partner. To her crazy mind, he can be the perfect date ever. He smells wonderful, holds her in his arms and makes her feel beautiful as the two glide around the room. This non-verbal communication between the two has led to the blooming of a whirlwind romance.

Trisha's recently started searching every single social media platform to stalk, learn more about him. ☺

Finally in contact with him through Facebook.

...

'What's up? Doing what?' T

'Nothing special. You say.' A

'Exams hanging over-head!' T

'Wt thn r u doin on Fb? U must b studyin' hard.' A

'Don't plz talk like my Mom-Dad.' T

'Who m I 2 talk like?' A

'Who u r?' T

'Who m I? *Hum aapke hein kaun?*' ☺ A

'Sm1 special for whom my heart beats like anything!' T

'Really?' A

'Hmmm. *Aazma lo.*' T

'*Aazmana toh chahta hun par...*' A

'*Par kya?*' T

'U r still too young! U r a babe. A chweeeet babe.' A

'That's why most fresh and wild.' T

'OMG!' A

'Wt hap?' T

'U r so tempting!' A

'So?' T

'Well...ummm...nothing. Let's see.' A

'A girl like me giving you *bhav* and u r mkn pretexts!' T

'I love it! I love...' A

'Lv wt?' T

'Lv everythn abt u.' A

'I'm worth it!!!' T

'Tomoro. What say?' A

'Tomoro's school.' T

'My wife wud b bk the day after that.' A

'Hmmm...'T

'Cn mk it?' A

'Wl hv 2. C ya!' T

...

...

It's one of the small flats in a grand building. Lot of construction work still on as it seems. A community swimming pool being dug perhaps. There're a number of labourers working around. A boy in uniform, watering plants.

Trisha gets down the bike.

She is still in school uniform.

Ameesh seems to have picked her up from the school.

'Take the keys. Flat no. 442, second floor. I'll be back in a couple of moments.'

'But...'

'Chill no? Don't trust me?'

'*Arrey* I do! What am I to do till then?'

'You'll get something on the bed. Try it till then.' he winks.

Trisha is so very excited.

Scared as well.

Should she run away?

Should she...?

Shouldn't...she?

...

She opens the room and has a close look of herself in the mirror first of all.

Satisfied, she sits on the edge of the bed and opens up the gift wrap lying on the bed as mentioned.

Her heart is galloping inside her chest walls.

Oh! It's so pretty! So very pretty! A short backless dress! It's jus' like one of her dream costumes which her Mum would never ever allow her to try even.

But...

Should she?

Shouldn't...she?

'There's nothing wrong dating someone jus' for the heck of it. All girls do such crazy wonderful things except for the nuns who have...no fun...like Anushka I hate the most!' she mumbles.

What if he wasn't trustworthy...after all...a guy...married too!

'What do I know about him besides the fact he's a charmer and the best dancer I've ever met?'

'May be...he has some camera hidden in the room?' she alarmingly moves around with the costume still in her hands.

'Don't be silly Trisha! Nothing wrong is *gonna* happen to you. Enjoy your day and forget it! Simple!'

'Think of the reactions your *besties* would give knowing this! After all you can't post this as your status update.' She finally shakes off all her maidenly fears and turns on the music.

All seems to have been well planned indeed for the song that plays, celebrates the personal stolen moments of love.

'Bhul gaya sab kuch, yaad nahin ab kuch, o ho

...

Julie...I love you...'

One of the songs that her Mom often launches into whenever she comes back home from somewhere or when she's working in the kitchen all by herself.

Not the right time to think of Mom!

...

A slight tap on the door.

Trisha opens the door hesitantly.

She has put on the beautiful dress.

Her uniform lies on the chair neatly piled up.

Ameesh beams.

Trisha responds warmly.

Ameesh opens his arms wide and Trisha sashays into them.

He runs his fingers over her cheeks, holding her face with utmost tenderness.

He doesn't seem to be in hurry to grab her to love at once.

He plans to ease into the gesture slowly and make it feel natural.

'I'll be back.' he whispers, nibbling at her ear lobe. He gently places a hand on the side of her face and strokes her cheek, her ear, her hair, her jawline while Trisha she shivers with a stolen joy.

'Enough of 'I'll be back'! Where r u *goin* now s.i.r...?' she cuddles around him.

'Five minutes? Need to change Sweet!' whispers Ameesh pushing into the area above her shoulder blades to knead out her tension and fear.

'Five minutes, okay?' Trisha hungers for more. Her throat goes dry with guilty excitement, her heart hot with a secret power. The power of love.

'Sure.'

Trisha adjusts the volume of the song, rewinds it to chime in the special moments...jumps onto the bed...

What freedom!

What tremendous sense of freedom!

That's what life is all about!

...

She will have a. t.h.i.n.g. to share with her diary and her friends!!!

...

...

Ameesh tosses her hair back to gently stroke her neck a little more down to the base of her shoulder and all the way up to her earlobe again.

Trisha gives a subtle smile feeling loved...

They curl together under a quilt.

Itnaa bhi door mat jaao ke paas aanaa mushkil ho
Itnaa bhi paas mat aaao ke door jaanaa mushkil ho

*****

19

The Guys Go Waxing!

'C'mon man! Even boys have the right to look good. What say?' Ronny seeks a nod of approval from his friends.

Ronny is all set for the farewell party which is soon to be there.

It would be his first date with Trisha.

Seemingly he is very-very excited.

'What's the plan?' asks Rishi, his bosom friend winking at him.

'Guys, you'll find it weird but...'

'But what you rascal? Out with it! You dog!' Rishi kicks his ass laughing.

'There must be something sweetly, deliciously crazy frying in your *bheja* pan! I can smell it!' Gaurav makes a funny sniffing sound.

'Ummm...I *wanna* have my arms and legs...'

'Waxed??!!!??' both ask in unison.

'W.e.l.l. y.e.s.!'

'*Oho!* Then put on a bikini and...'

'Shut up!'

'You know what? You are right, man! We'll buy you a beautiful dress with a deep cleavage and before that we don't mind you waxing h.e.r.e. too.' they double with laughter, running their hands over his chest hair.

'Noooo! Any hair but these! Thou can't touch it you wretched fellows! Thou are slain if...' Ronny bursts into laughter.

He rolls on the floor pressing his tummy.

Rishi mounts upon him and sings... *'ye mera dil...'*

'Saale kaminon! Tum kisi kaam ke nahin ho. Dost ki madad toh nahin kar sakte.' Ronny pushes Rishi away pretending to be annoyed.

...

'Gimme your mobile.' Ronny reaches for Gaurav's pocket.

'Why? Where's yours?'

'That's long story.' Ronny pulls a long face.

'We don't mind listening.'

'The world is running super-fast and I don't have a smart phone! *Ektualllly...*Dad bought me a 'Samsung Galaxy Y' last year. All my friends had 3G phones with quad cores and I used to be damn jealous you know...so...one day I flushed it in the toilet.'

'Whaaat!!!'

'Aage toh sun. I came out with expressions of remorse.'

'Sounds interesting! *Phir?'*

'I explained...it had happened by mistake. I explained that one couldn't survive without a smart phone in this super- fast techno world. So they could buy me an android and that...I was ready to wait for a month if they wanted.'

'Saale kameene! Phir kya hua?'

'Leave it man! You know how my Dad is...he consoled me... hiding his grin...a.n.d. sang a l.o.n.g. s.o.r.r.r.y.'

'Super *beijjaati yaar!'*

'Know what Rishi? This dog has been sharing my personal number with all his gals and I'm sick of attending their WhatsApp – *mein kaunse sandals khareedu? Ye colour mere dress ke saath jayega kya nahin?* But I jus' love, love, love the...yummy non-vegetarian chats late night...'

'*Saale iska matlab tu...*'Ronny hurls abuses at Gaurav.

'If you publicise my number, shouldn't I be paid in return? You know what? Trisha sounds damn delicious past midnight!' Gaurav teases Ronny.

'Cool down! He's kidding *yaar!*' Rishi intervenes as they roll up their sleeves for a fresh bout of encounter.

'*Vaise bhi ladki patana iske bas ki baat nahin hai. Phenkta hai saala. Saala...* for nine long years...after the same girl...AND she is always asking other guys out!' Rishi says.

Silence falls.

Gaurav goes touchy at the very mention of the girl he loves. His face at once shrinks like he'd bitten into a bitter fruit. It was since the times when he didn't actually know the meaning of the word LOVE.

'U know what? U r a sentimental fool! That's what you are! She doesn't deserve you, damn it! More than that...you *saala* don't deserve a girl at all. Frankly speaking, sometimes I fear if you are a gay or what?'

'Shut up!'

'We think what we think unless you prove us wrong.' laugh Rishi and Ronny.

...

Rishi is presently back from the kitchen carrying a tea-pan with steaming water.

There is a freshly opened pack of readymade wax stripes lying nearby.

Ronny has slipped into his shorts for the purpose.

YouTube is on with the search result- How to do waxing...

Male Body **Waxing, Waxing** for **Men** - YouTube
▶ 5:49 ▶ 5:49
www.youtube.com/watch?v=0abc1pq3rxyz45

Jan 14, 2015 - Uploaded by XYZ

Waxing is a hair removal trend for **men** that involves spreading hot ... YouTube **home** ... Within a few days ...

Rishi applies steaming hot wax on Ronny's leg while Gaurav blows out some air from his mouth to cool it down on the way.

The soon to be men r at serious business.

No smile on their faces.

Ronny presses his lips together to contain himself...

...can't contain however the moment Rishi pulls the stripe with a jungle of hair.

"Yuck! What the hell!" Ronny exclaims with repulsion.

Slap!!!

'Saale! Ek baar mein maar daalega kya?'

'Toh tu sochta hai ki sexy legs yunhi??? Saala!' Rishi screams.

*****

20

Trisha is Not a Problem! Teenage is

'Ragini darling! I told you not to mess with her.'

'Mess with her? She's my daughter Akshay! Even Nikki's Mom says that Nikki has been staying out too late these days. And that the girl talks back if questioned! She treats her mother like dirt...I was a fool to believe that...'

'Ragini plz. Let's not compare.'

'I was a fool to believe that my family was immune to teenage problems. I was a fool to say-'*Phew. Not my Trisha...*' Ragini laughs an acid laugh.

'*Ufff!* Crying is not the solution honey. *Trisha is not a problem! Teenage is!* Like...one minute she is your darling daughter begging you to come on the class trip with her or lie down with her till she falls asleep...and then...then seemingly overnight... things change right?'

'Yes. That's what is happening Akshay! She starts discounting everything I say and snickers at my suggestions.' Ragini is apparently very agitated.

'If you look closely darling, you'll realize that we've been through all this even before this teenage knocked upon the door...remember how when she was still a toddler and later when a school goer... she would shout '*No*' when she didn't like something we said?'

'And...now as a teenager she simply rolls her eyes in disgust. I just don't understand. When she's home, she's often sleeping in. She has no time for me.' Ragini adds tartly.

'She isn't lazy I tell you dear. Teenagers love to sleep in. I read it somewhere the other day. It's the way their bodies are programmed dear. It's a hormone called pro melatonin that helps them fall asleep. That's why they are champion snoozers you know! Ha ha!'

'I need no scientific clarifications about her behaviour. I behave friendly with her. I see to it that all her demands are satisfied. She's stopped sharing things with me. It's always she and her diary. So...' she hesitates.

'...you read her personal diary?' asks Akshay.

'Yes.'

'Ragini! You shouldn't have! I mean this is not right!'

'How could I know otherwise what was going on in her crazy mind?'

'What did you exactly do?' Akshay asks, bewildered.

'I tried to extract a confession from her.'

'What confession for God's sake?' Akshay tries to register her tone.

'Well...about her menstrual cycle.'

'Theek hai theek hai...' the ground seems to have tilted under his feet.

'I suspected...she was missing her periods...'

'!!!' he is stupefied, reaches out to the nearest table and holds it tight.

'I had to know.'

'???'

'...she screamed and wept saying I didn't trust her...BUT I wasn't convinced. So, I sifted through her mails and diary...'

'It was wrong, I say.'

'Do you understand what could this mean?'

'I understand nothing. It's such an invasion! And...you have been caught! It may take a long time to rebuild the trust and credibility again.' he weighs each word he speaks.

'To hell with the trust! What if she is actually pregnant Akshay? Now you read yourself.' she hands over Trisha's personal diary to him.

'Now for God's sake, what's thisss?' he asks horrified.

It reads-

'*M* worried. *M* worried beyond words dear. *M* missing my periods! God knows what's happening! Looks like I'm gone! Although I had resolved to stay abstinent until I was married...but...I had my questions you know. *I did wonder*...you know...and *I had my queries*...questions I might get grounded for if I asked at home... that's why...dear diary...that's why I went off like my classmates and had sex...with...well, u know him well...mi dance teacher. He charms me like anythn! I was driven crazy by the things in my head...And...things are never like my parents see at home. At home I'm all good...though at times with Mom...it just happens. I don't cuss and I do chores as told by Mum or Dad but in schools things go different. We cuss and ditch classes...our parents grew up in times when sex was a taboo. It was meant for rebels alone... but now...I walk around school...can see gals who are carrying... their boyfriends pick them up from outside the school gate to take them to the doctor to get an abortion done and...if not so...the girls are getting information from all odd sources about being a Mom...

We are teens! We are exploring a dangerous territory called teenage. That too without a map! Oh! It's a maze of intense emotions! We have much to share if only grown-ups listened. And much to hide so easily-if only grown-ups were not so blind...hope none finds out.

Please God! Save me this time. I swear. I'll be a good girl. If only I have my periods back before...'

...

'Leave me alone for a while Ragini.' Akshay pleads with wet eyes.

'I'm scared Akshay.'

'Now I'm scared too.'

*****

21

The Irrevocable Slip

'Mom how can I live without *mi* mobile? I mean without my contacts?' Trisha is highly-highly upset as it seems.

'Your contacts have landed us in the soup. You don't deserve the liberty we gave you.'

'Okay fine. I won't be begging any further.' says Trisha disdainfully.

'You had better not.'

'Can I call my friends home? Plz?'

'No!'

'???'

'That's how it is going to be.'

'Am I allowed to b.r.e.a.t.h.e...OR NOT?'

'Trisha we love you darling! Don't be so rude! Mom loves you!' Ragini advances to hug her.

'Stay away!' Trisha screams in anger and pain.

'Trisha!'

...

A few hours later...

...

The sun has packed over the horizon.

...

The world outside the room's window is growing an eerie blue melded with a few beautiful strokes of red.

Crimson light spills in and it's a halo around Trisha's head.

She looks very innocent and beautiful.

Trisha leans over her mother's shoulder and is apparently too agonized to speak a word.

She just cries inconsolably in her arms.

The moment could be a pinnacle of their lives had things not gone the wrong way.

'You are my life Trisha! You are my dream! Holding you in my fond motherly arms is more natural to me than my own heart beat! My heart is filled with a unique pleasure seeing you growing each day but...' a knot twists in her stomach.

Trisha doesn't respond. She just stares into nothingness until their breathing coincides.

'Hope you know how much you mean to us?' the mother strokes daughter's head warmly.

'Mom!'

'Hmm?'

'Perhaps I've gone the wrong way Mom. Perhaps I shouldn't have. Perhaps this was not the right time to...' Trisha's fingers are tracing invisible circles slowly over her Mom's hand...

The two dissolve into passion.

Like magic...theirs years apart don't matter for the moment.

'Baby listen! You're supposed to be changing the world! Not changing diapers! Enjoy your youth *by being a kid, not raising one!* Now c'mon! Get up. It's evening time. Will you come with me to pray?' asks Ragini, rubbing her palm.

'My questions are yet to be answered Mom.' Trisha smiles a wry smile.

'No more questions. Come.' Ragini resolves to be soft.

'I'm sorry. I need answers first.' Trisha is visibly trying to push her filial emotions back.

'What's wrong with you child?' Ragini seems at the verge of losing her patience once more.

'Why can't I have my mobile? And how am I going to study if you don't let me go to school?'

'Okay. Tell me one thing - are you really concerned about that dear?'

'Again you are suspecting me *naa?*'

'Yes. I am.'

They are going to give it another shot as it seems.

Silence...

...

...

Trisha's mind drifts through the last few weeks.

'I love him.' announces Trisha, glancing away.

'You must be out of your senses! Get a hold of yourself!' the mother can contain no longer.

...

It's so easy to teach a mother how she should behave with her children.

It's so difficult; so very difficult to be a mother.

Trisha is fiery, passionate and daring.

'We'll talk tomorrow. Tomorrow we'll be seeing the doctor as well.' notifies the mother.

'I need no doctor. Don't bother Mom. I've done the home pregnancy test. AND IT IS NEGATIVE.'

Ragini can't dwell on the subject any longer.

She wonders at the ease Trisha talks about it.

Talks about pregnancy!

A teenager as such!

So immature outwardly!

Ragini's hasty steps towards the porch betray her internal disquiet.

...

...

It's been a week almost Trisha hasn't moved out of her room.

She can't contact her friends.

She can't talk to the man of her dreams.

She can't tell Ronny that there would be no dating ever between the two.

No diary even! The only bosom friend of hers.

...

...

She has her PC on.

A blank page is all that she needs when she is so agitated inside; when there's an effervescence of feelings she can't hold.

'Hi diary! Hope you don't mind this electronic mode. I hate it! I hate the days! Hate them like anything! Couldn't imagine all this! Even I'm wondering why am I missing my periods if...if it is not the damned pregnancy thing. Gargy, one of my good friends I shared this secret with, said...it happens sometimes in teenage... when we take too much stress of studies or...*well I'm unknown to that stress...*I leave it for book worms like Anushka...hmm...or when we work overnights...*dunno* what's the reason...may be junk food in my case but thank God...it's not pregnancy! I'm sure Dad's anger will subside in a few more days. It's a mild storm you know. Dad is not that hard to deal with. I'll break this ominous silence and draw the poison out of him. And then...hopefully things would be back to normal...know what? I hate my friends too. None of them has come to inquire why am I going absent. For a week! They must be fearing interrogation. Damn it! They all know my secrets. Well, do you think I should terminate my relationship with *him?* Take it as it is...*him*...I mean I can't write the name. AND I can't realllllly say that I'm emotionally attached to *him.* There isn't anything like that. It was just...infatuation I think. Can't really describe things I have been through...'

Trisha digs her face into the soft pillow.

Streams of tears roll down her face.

No-body has spoken to her the entire day.

She has been confined to the room.

The crushing weight of walls is killing her inside.

The screen opens up blank on a Facebook Page-

Update status-   **Add photos/Video**

'What's on your mind?'

...

'Watching someone you love walk away from you, while you stand there saying 'Please don't go...'is so painful! Someone, the one you thought would protect you is the one who hurts you the most! Vaise u should be punched in the face multiple times. You r a dirty rotten liar n I wish I had never met u. Don' wanna b my frnd anymo'e? Haha! I DON'T GIVE A SHIT! U didn't deserve me anyway. Hv a nice life! **** YOU!

But I miss u! I hate to admit this but...I miss u! Truly! You must be hvn ur wife in ur arms ri8 now...like you loved me that day... whispering sugary things in bed, by my side... while I'm all tears and sighs...u rogue! I HATE YOU!'

Post

It's not long before she realises what she's done...OMG! OMG!!! She was to post all that rubbish not as status update but as a personal message to him!!!

She is panicky waiting for Facebook to re-open.

That's what she feared!!!

Lots of comments pouring in!

Like. Comment. Share.

Write a comment...

83 people like this.

Ronney- You sexy little girl! I always knew what you were up to. Now suffer!

Sujoy- I'm enjoying it you know? I'm enjoying it! Before you have a Bachelor's Degree in hand, you have a lover in bed! May be a child spewing in your lap! Great going haan!'

Dev- The first thing to share in the school tomorrow! Vaise I wonder who doesn't know it!

Preity- Trapped haan! You always wanted a whirlwind romance, we knew...but a married man...shit yaar!

Natasha- Girl! How many dates do you think you can handle at a time?

Nikki-If I'm not wrong it was dirty dance that led you to the hot waters darling...eh...?

Ajeet- Ek chance hamen bhi deke dekhti.

...

...

...

'Well, I am undone! Can't think of going to school ever again!'

She deletes the post at once *but the humiliation that she has suffered...will linger on with her name...for how long...God* knows. She would probably never be able to squirm out from this load of humiliation and go back to school.

Great, racking sobs erupt from her.

She hasn't wept like this for years.

*****

22

Pack-up

'I don't wanna stay here anymore. Dad please! Get me admitted to some hostel.'

'Doll, we don't want to!'

'For God's sake! Why is it always *you guys* who want to or don't want to? What about me? Does anybody care in this house what I want?'

'We care for you that's why we don't want you to...'adds Ragini.

'But I can't live like a mouse in a hole. Hope you guys understand?'

'We do understand but...you have actually left us with no choice dear.' Akshay is at a loss of words.

'Fine! FINE! I'll see then what I have to do.'

'Trisha!'

Trisha walks out.

'This girl...!!!' the mother is distraught.

'Calm down dear. Let's try to think from her point of view.' counsels the father.

'And overlook what she's done? Can you close your eyes to the disgrace Akshay?'

'I think we are going too hard on her. She may retaliate. Let's not make it an issue bigger than it is.'

'???'

'I understand Ragini. What she's done is unpardonable but thank God!'

'Yes! The stigma might've robbed us of all we have!'

'Hmmm...I do want that she learns to be disciplined. I think hostel is not that bad an idea. *To the teens, life is techno coloured. To elders their world is sensitive, moody and often dangerous. As their hormones kick into high gear, they go from feeling maniac and on the top of the world to crestfallen and at the bottom of the barrel, in a matter of moments.*' Akshay wisely adds holding his wife's gaze until she nods.

'But I'm scared Akshay.'

'Need not be. Let me gather some details about some good hostels. If she stays here, she might be tempted again. That bastard can cajole her again. Never dreamt of the days!'

*****

23

Is a U-Turn Possible?

'*Tune suna yaar*? Don't know *yeh sab aakhir ho kya raha hai!*' exclaims Anurag.

'*Bataaega bhi?*' Rohan asks nonchalantly as he slouches comfortably, watching some YouTube video.

'Read this. The suicide of a DU girl. She's left behind a voice note how she was driven to the drastic step.' says Anurag.

'A psychopathic romantic lover *haan!*' chuckles Rohan, his eyes still glued to the Tablet.

'*Saale tujhme kuch feelings veelings hein ya nahin?* What if she were your sis?'

'*Teri sis thi kya? Tu kyun itna senti ho raha hai yaar?*' Rohan asks dispassionately.

Anurag's eyes are wet.

'*Arrey kya hua?*'

'What to tell man! The same happened to one of my close friend's sis *yaar*. Hardly a month ago. *Vo mujhe bhi bhai manati thi. Rakhi bandhti thi.*'

'Well, *kya hua tha?*'

'She was an under-graduate DU girl. A guy began stalking her. He'd chase her in the broad daylight; harass her even at nights by sending messages, videos and MMSs on her mobile. He would call her incessantly...and...'

'Scoundrel! Why didn't she complain against him? Or she could've shared with her parents, no?'

'She got his number blocked. She lived in a girls' hostel where there was no male entry possible. One night when she returned, she found some obscene love notes on the walls of her room. She was naturally scared wondering how could he manage to get in. It looked like he had bribed the warden. She was scared if she told her parents, they wouldn't allow her to study further so...she returned home on the pretext of homesickness but...the nightmare didn't end there.'

'I still think she should've told her parents.' Rohan concludes putting the video in mute mode.

'It's not that easy Rohan. Most of the girls who face such nasty situations living in cosmopolitans as PGs, they just keep adding such Road-side Romeos to the blocked contact number lists. That's what they can instinctively think of. Not reporting the matter about the stocker may seem dumb to you or anyone else but...filing a complaint makes things worse at times.'

'Well yes. You remind me of news I recently read. It was about a student who brutally assaulted his girl classmate with an axe inside a classroom and then...killed himself! India blindly following West! A few days back, the US saw yet another horrifying gun massacre by a twenty-two-year-old-collegiate. His frustration was the same millions of young people face across the globe today- failing to win dates. Failing to win dates man! It's somehow directly related to America's all too lax gun rules that make arms as easily available as candies...whatever be the instrument of death...it's the girl that suffers the most! I can understand *yaar!*'

'Let's move out of this 10*10 room that suffocates especially in weather like this! It's all so clammy! I hate rains you know. Let's have some fresh air.' mumbles Anurag in a voice choked with tears.

'Aaj maa ki badi yaad aa rahi hai yaar!' says Rohan.

'Why don't you go home for a couple of days? It would recharge your batteries man!' suggests Anurag.

'How am I going to face them? How am I to hide the fact that I can't live without drugs even for 24 hours? What if they again take me to the therapist and she is able to detect the drugs running in my blood? They would be shattered *yaar!*' Rohan mumbles.

'Parents are such poor sentimental things!' Anurag adds with compunction in his voice.

The sky outside has cleared.

No more clouds.

They lock the door and look for a taxi but finally decide to walk.

The hills at distance and the trees around look freshly bathed and sparkling clean.

Their faces are radiant with a new hope.

'I.s. t.h.i.s...j.u.s.t. p.o.s.s.i.b.l.e...I mean if I could do a U-turn...I mean if I could somehow get rid of this vicious circle? It was all so good a life when I was cocooned by parents and teachers and the urge to slip out of it seemed such a far off possibility! It was only when the big words like AMBITION, COMPETITIVE EXAMS, CAREER, SUCCESS, CHALLENGES, FAT PACKAGES and the like lunged at my mind that the game began...' mutters Rohan in a voice wet with regret and pain. His face wears strange expressions. His feet as if have nothing to do with the path. They are eager to move away from it.

'*Hota hai yaar!* That's what life is all about. Remember the story-'*Rat-trap?*'

'Well yes. Temptations! Why do people go gaga over this kind of stuff? I mean, why can't you be satisfied with a lower package but a peaceful life; with a girl of your choice in arms and the little joys that you often miss on running after the big things?'

'I never knew you were a philosopher too!' Anurag tries to talk animatedly.

'Am I?' Rohan cocks an amused eyebrow at Anurag.

'You are!'

Their hearts back to equilibrium.

Perhaps.

A whiff of sharp wind untamed, stirs their whole beings.

'Missing someone else now?' Anurag asks with a smirk.

'Haan yaar! Kabhi kabhi mere dil mein khayal aata hai...'

*****

24

Back to the School

Truth and Dare

The school Trisha has left behind suffers no change whatsoever. It will go on as usual with or without the pranksters, with or without the studious ones, with or without any particular teacher or even with or without the Principal. It has seen many generations of pupils properly tuning in with its ambience, swimming in its pool, playing and swinging in the vast grounds, chit-chatting in its canteen, hatching little conspiracies against each other, enjoying their tiffin under shady trees, standing in long queues for buses and above all extracting the best out of their childhood and adolescence.

This world has constructed *a world within* to these children that no external threat can penetrate till they have passed out from here and entered *the world outside this world.* It is then that the cut throat competition and bitterness of frustrated dreams begin their irrevocable work. It is then that they face and feel hatred 'n' love, despair 'n' tedium, 'n' all those simple yet foolish things that go into the making of everyday life...

These pupils are therefore prepared here to be strong enough to clamber up these walls and peer over at the stronger world outside.

It is October going on. Diwali holidays are round the corner. This phase of the year has been a perennial source of fascination for students for this is the time they can prove their mettle by playing dangerous pranks upon the school authorities i.e. bursting crackers in the school's grounds and thus flying in the teeth of all instructions imparted.

...

School assembly is going on.

The principal is seen on the stage with his usual lectures...and all.

'I have been telling you students about unconditional love we provide you. Back then in our time there used to be lot of respect in the hearts of children for their teachers and they would touch their feet in reverence as a matter of rule whenever and wherever they met them....' he drones on.

'Oh not again! *Hamare zamane mein toh*...!' Nikki yawns.

Students look here and there in awe as the Princi has suddenly stopped in the middle of speaking. He hasn't actually stopped. It's one of his favourite little pauses to gather what impression his speech has had on them. He finds a few students giggling and nudging and a few pretending to have dozed off and snoring soft.

'I'm encouraged to speak further on behalf of those who are all ears to me. AND for those...who couldn't have a sound sleep last night, let me repeat...this Diwali we aren't going to burst any crackers even at home...not to speak of school surroundings alone.'

'What the hell Diwali is for if we can't...? Now we have to wait for Holi to burst crackers, right?' whispers Ronny in her ears.

'Right!' laughs Nikki.

'I always am!' beams Ronny.

...

...

'Dear Diary

I was looking forward to some fantabulous plan from the seniors' side regarding Princi's restrictions about crackers and all. They did come out with *toofani planz!* Of course I supported them! Except me, Ronny and a few other juniors, nobody had an idea what was going to happen in the recess.

Shhh...! My role was to provide them the arms...:)

So, what I did...was very simple. I searched for some left over crackers from the last Diwali at home, did find them, wore an additional pair of shorts beneath the ones I usually do, kept a few *sootli* bombs inside and thus escaped the stupid bag-check round we have been undergoing for a couple of days after assembly.

You know what? Hee-hee. I was actually scared what if they burst in my shorts on their own accord! Stupid fears! Nothing happened.

I was in my group in the senior block having lunch, cracking jokes and the usual silly stuff...and suddenly a booooooom!!! All glass windows in the rooms went like...*khad-khad-khad*...It took others a few minutes to understand what was actually happening. ...I was pretty aware what was happening... ;) all rushed towards the boys' washroom where the sound travelled from. I felt so innocent wearing a look of one, dumb with surprise. Oh! How I missed Trisha! We'd have gone mad wd laughter till our tears trickled down our cheeks...wish...her Mom n Dad have a lil pity on her and they finally let her join the school again.

Well...I'm keeping a secret frm her...m afraid...if she comes back...Ronny and me...you know what I mean...so...better if she doesn't.

Thank God! The Princi was absent today or he'd surely have suspended the boys. He'll be there tomorrow. Let's C...we are in for a live 'Truth and Dare'. I know. I know. U'll be curious 4 further details. Tell you what? I'm carrying u 2 school 2morro...of course for the latest updates...☺

Gud ni8...

...

...

Hi,

No time 4 formal greetings. You know what happened? How would you? K fine. Let me tell ya. The Princi did give them a piece of his mind. He said he'd go 2 the depth and find out who after all provided the stuff...shhhh...three of the boys have been suspended. *Ektuallly* suspended you know!

Wait!

Something is happening outside...

...OMG! Not again! It's been a double blast! One near the Maths Lab and the other between the gaps of two blocks! Nobody is allowed in the corridor. It's just like...curfew you know. Senior teachers r taking rounds to find out the root elements behind the entire mess. Oh! The word *'mess'* makes me go...go...*kinda* mad you know...I love all kinds of *mess* since I've fallen in love with Lionel Messi. How cool he looks in those shorts! What a player *yaar!*

Sry sry...there has been a circular that there will be an anti-cracker rally tomorrow evening. Everybody saying- *what rubbish!'*

...

...

'Hi Dear,

Here is your faithful friend @ your service again. I've just returned from the so called rally. I'd have said no but for the temptation... Ronny suggested that we went by his scooty...2gether u know! Trisha was right! HE IS MAGNETIC! We were enjoying the proximity which we rarely have in school. The seniors, apart from the ones involved in the rally, cracked bombs there itself! It was a *mess* again! Hee-hee.

The rally was cancelled.

I'm waiting for the school to re-open.

I'm waiting to know what happens next.

Happy Diwali!

Yours

...

...

Hi again,

Have I changed more than I think? Am I kidding myself? Reading it all again what I have written in you till today, is very revealing. It makes me cringe, as well as laugh, several times. I have changed in some ways, not in others. I sometimes feel a lot less worthy and less sure about myself than I used to be. What is it about Trisha that she has such charisma? I know she's very pretty and friendly but...I really don't think she's amazing, you know. She's my best friend but I can't help feeling jealous sometimes, especially when we meet new people. I feel inferior and inadequate.

Now she's gone, so lemme not think so much about her. I should be confident of my looks and my relationships now. Now onto more serious stuff. Ronny likes me. Earlier I used to fixate on a new boy on weekly basis. Losing my virginity is in the headlines. Shhh...HE IS MAGNETIC!

*****

25

Are 'Mean Gals' Real?

A Crush Defined

Trisha has reached the hostel.

A four hours' drive from her home town.

She is awestruck by the beautiful infrastructure. It's a line of high tech buildings with various blocks for academics and hostels. In each block there's a central open area where there's either a garden or playground or lot of open space to hang out. There's also a book shop where you can buy all sorts of books and there are really nice stationary shops. All the buildings are centrally air-conditioned and all the facilities that may ever be needed in a school are there. There is a big library with ample of books apart from something called an e-library which can be accessed through the school internet. There's Wi-Fi connectivity all over the campus but when everyone is simultaneously online, the net speed is terribly reduced due to bandwidth sharing.

The school provides excellent hostel facilities and makes sure that all those who need accommodation get one. The hostels are like residential apartments and the rooms are very well furnished. The rooms are available as single or 2/3/4 sharing and you've to pay accordingly.

Presently there are two more girls with Trisha in the room allotted.

...

'Open the door!' someone shouts from outside.

'What's up? We are dressing Miss.' Trisha's room-mates answer from within cautioning each other to pack things fast.

'No excuses please! Open the door! Right now!'

'You will do nothing but ogle us like a boob?' Trisha's roommates shoot her questioning looks.

'Wh...what am I supposed to? Open the door?' asks Trisha helplessly.

'You idiot! You just sit here and relax!' Trisha is pushed aside.

She is at once cowed down.

'Will someone tell me what's happening here? Please?' Trisha whispers back.

The girls move about in a flash. One hides the hair dryer, the electric kettle, the iron board, their trendy mobiles-n-all in a bag and pushes it under the bed while the other opens a big piece of cloth, hastily places packs of cigarettes and alcohol in it, ties a tight knot and hangs it outside the window. She then moves towards the door humming like...nothing happened. She re-settles her top and denims pretending that she's just done with her dressing.

'Get aside! Why so much time taken to open the door? What have you been up to?' the fat warden smells the situation.

'We were going out for a stroll in the ground ma'am. Dressing up. We told you.'

'Dressing up...hmm...has someone been smoking again?' the warden growls sniffing like a spy dog.

'No ma'am! We promised you we wouldn't ever...'

'Take heed! I won't be melted by your tears this time. You'll be thrown out of the hostel the day you're caught red handed. I can tolerate anything but a thing that brings our hostel a bad name.'

'Yessss ma'am!' the two blurt out in unison.

...

'What was all that?' Trisha asks.

'A regular raid. What else?'

'What if the things you hid, got confiscated?'

'They can be procured on recommendation. What else? Easy!'

...

It's been a fortnight.

Trisha is picking up the manners and mannerism of the place.

She more or less feels herself to be a soldier who is on warfront having left the comforts of home behind in pursuit of a better life.

'Ma'am I've lost mi mobile. I'd left it on the study table only a few hours back.' complains Trisha, pulling a long face.

'A few hours? Don't tell me there is a teenager who keeps away from his/her mobile for a. f.e.w. h.o.u.r.s!!!' the warden pooh-poohs.

'But ma'am? How am I to...?'

'Don't panic. *Lemme* see.' assures the warden entering the room and throwing an inquisitive glance at the room-mates.

'Well, we *dunno* anything. We've been preparing our lessons you know.' the girls nonchalantly respond.

'Okay then. Let me find it out myself.' says the latter tossing their books and registers into a mess.

'Here it is.' declares Ananya, one of the two room-mates of Trisha.

'See? Now take care. A lot of crazy shit goes on here.' warns the warden.

'What do you mean by crazy shit ma'am?' Trisha asks intrigued.

'You need not the theory. They'll teach you in practical.'

Ananya and the other girl, named Navya, burst into laughter.

Trisha joins them too.

'*Mera* phone *kyon chupaya? Bolo!*' asks Trisha in a childlike manner.

'We couldn't hear you all the time telling your *Mumma* that you were missing her. A *kiddo!*'

'*Mumma's* doll.'

'Why did you come here if you needed your Ma to sleep with?' winks Ananya.

'Who do you want to sleep with?' asks Trisha, amused.

'A dusky muscular lover.'

'OMG!'

'What OMG? Have you never ever fallen in love?'

'Well, not yet.' answers Trisha.

One of the biggest relationship lessons Trisha has learned is that some things should just be kept to oneself. When a girl is not so happy with a guy, she is way more likely to vent to her friends 24/7, or ask them to help her analyse every text and interaction to see what they thought it meant. It's normal to want to talk about one's boyfriend, but when she feels like she constantly has BF problems to talk about instead of anything else, that's a pretty bad sign.

...

'Then ask me how it feels like. I can give you the step by step detail of having a CRUSH.'

'Please do that.'

'Interested *haan?*'

'I really am.' Trisha glows.

'See, it is like...you like someone and you can't *ekchullly* breathe in his presence around! You wear your heart on sleeves and decide you would tell him but then you miserably fail each time you try.'

'Hmm?'

'...and then one day he finally asks u to borrow a pencil~ and you are like ~this is the first day of my life~'

'Well...?'

'...u try to play it cool when he talks to u, but u *smhw* always end up embarrassing *urself*...u finally exchange numbers to 'study' for the next exam together...'

'And...?'

'...and when he finally sends you the first text...you are like~ OMG! I AM DEAD!!! And u completely forget how to speak.'

'Heehee! *Aagey?*'

'*U* start hanging out outside the school and *u r* pretty sure he is~ you know~ going to~ make a move.'

'Then...?' Trisha giggles, unable to control her laughter any more.

'Don't ask further.' Navya interrupts.

'Tell me no?'

'Fine! If you insist...here we go...then...mmm...then one day you hear his friend talking about his *new boo* whom he met at the mall last week...and you are like, 'wait, WHAT?!? I sweetly thought something was going on between me and him???''

'Sad.' Trisha gives her favourite Alia Bhatt kinda expression.

'And then u see him at the mall with the girl you heard about one weekend and you are like 'ARE YOU FREAKIN KIDDIN ME???''

'Bad.'

'*Arrey yaar* there's nothing sad or bad about it. You decide to move on...you are like, 'WHATEVER! HE WAS CUTE BUT HE WASN'T **THAT CUTE** ~ NEXT.'

'Heehee.'

Trisha is attracted to these girls more and more. You'll at once want to be friends with Ananya who's got her priorities straight; beautiful clothing and a love for '*Mean Girls*', and a dedication to sunshine. Say what u want about her but the gal knows how to wear an outfit. Her ultimate blend of brands and '*I don't give a fuck what my age is'* attitude has catapulted her into the fashion world.

For most of Ananya's sixteen years of life, she was 'a normal kid' who swam on the school swim team and looked forward to family trips every year. She enjoyed all her classes and her classmates. Drugs and alcohol had never been a problem. 'I didn't drink or smoke,' she says. But her boyfriend was another story. 'My boyfriend was into heroin,' she says. He tempted her many a times but she never did. And then a year ago, he jabbed her with a heroin-filled syringe as she walked by. 'I was shocked~ at first~ then I grew to need the drug.' It wasn't long that Ananya became an addict. 'I would use once every couple of weeks' she says. 'But then it progressed...and I was doing it every day.' She was stealing money from her parents to buy drugs.

All lying, stealing and stress led to a horrible breakdown. Neither she nor her family could stand things as they were.

Ananya was to be supported no doubt as best as she could be but...there were three younger sisters who had to be saved from the influence.

There was one solution.

Hostel.

Navya is a free birdie who unlike other school goers doesn't feel pressurized at all to look like her peers. She in fact loves 'dressing weird' and is a self-proclaimed freak. She is beautifully capable to put together different textures and play cool with them.

She couldn't however do anything but play an accomplice when Ananya after a long phase of sobriety returned to her daily drugs. Ananya assisted by Navya, brought drugs and needles for a four-day senior retreat. But the school staff discovered their plans and called their parents to pick them up. Both fell to their knees to be given jus' one more chance.

The warden outwardly stern is a soft hearted woman in fact. They weren't expelled from the school.

It's been months of shy graduating since then.

...

Trisha?

She's in the learning phase. She uses urban street style as a jumping off point and adds her own spin on it to create something really unique and out of the box.

...

Tuesday April 27th

Dear Diary

It's really scary how life is passing me by so quickly. It seems like yesterday when I was eleven but a few years ahead I can see myself nineteen or twenty. Guess what? I often wonder what the purpose of my life is. I know that to be content I need to achieve something in my life. I want to be remembered, to attain some goal, to be loved intense, to be appreciated...otherwise my life will be a waste. Meeting new friends has never made me happier for you know what kind of a state of mind I'm trying to move out from. I haven't enjoyed myself so much for ages. Both Ananya and Navya are jus' terrific! And yes! I don't fancy Amish anymo.

Trisha

*****

26

Delhi Diaries-

'I have been to Delhi quite a number of times and it is not a new place for me. This time however it is altogether a new sight, a brighter way, wider city and a fresh new perspective for after all I am a college boy now.

...well...

Getting off the bus near my college.

Walking to the college.

It's the first week...of the first year.

I hear some-one calling me from behind.

It's a senior.

He asks me to introduce myself.

He tries to grill me on everything I say.

He doesn't like my attitude.

Attitude?

Do I have attitude?

But *maine aisa kya kiya!*

He is freshly joined by a few more.

I'm a little scared.

They accuse me of not respecting my seniors.

They finally ask me to memorise names of all my 108 batch mates with their hometowns.

Within a week.

I'm in my room making a list.

They want me and my room-mates not to use the elevator to our class rooms.

So that we may know *ki* what actually exists on every floor in the college.

We do observe that the accommodations are given on pretty selective basis. Like the first floor is reserved for first year scholars only. This, to my mind, may be in order to reduce the scope for ragging.

They don't allow us to go to the canteen.

They expect us to do ramp-walk for them on the fresher's day.

At midnight, November 21 they pour cold water on us and ask us to do all sorts of acts and dances.

To act gay for them.

Some fresher ones are made to have sex with a goat.

(School of planning and architecture.)

I did read somewhere that during ragging some poor fresher ones had to do sit-ups with bricks on their heads. They had suffered fractures.

I fear what next, with us!

...

...

Their faces beam with satisfaction.

Contrary to what we apprehend, they give us warm hugs and a promise to help us with all our problems!!!

They actually act like guardians to us from the very day onwards.

...

College life is GR8.

It's random fun; you are exposed to all new things- sudden freedom and a sudden sense of independence.

First year.

Two classes. Two hours' break. Two more classes.

Four hours' bunk. ;)

It becomes a habit, you know, with most of us.

Attendance is necessary, no doubt.

But you learn the game.

You have connections.

So attendance?

No problem.

Shaam hote hi you go back home.

U have friends *jinke saath* u go out clubbing in the nights. Stay out all night. Eat and drink. Your friends are always ready for drinking and doping.

They always need small *sutta* breaks.

They are the chimneys releasing their pressures in the form of smoke.

There are a few however *jinke ki liye* going to library in every free period is a ritual they religiously follow. It is like- one hour class- library- detailed studies-class-library- detailed studies...

There are gyms. The need to have a good muscular body is the basic requisite. There are brand marks. There's rivalry between trainers. Girls first look at the trainers' beefy bodies and then decide who to join.

Lot of hooking-up going on everywhere.

Here too obviously.

There are *sm khool* teachers u like being with. U love their classes and talking to them as well.

And there are those strict ones who are always behind *ur* ass.

U have the hunks in the colleges always surrounded by people. They are the college idols, so to say. They are heroes with classy gals around them. Every second girl has a crush on them.

There're *Richy Rich* kinds who throw gala parties. Money spent like- in lakhs over these liquor parties! Maximum number of scholars invited. There are groups. There is rivalry as who can spend more. These guys would love to count the cash only when a beautiful girl passes their way.

You hangout.

Try new things.

Fall in love.

Fall out of love.

On your Facebook account your status keeps changing- **Single- Committed- Single...**

AT MOST YOU CAN ENJOY A WEEKLY RELATIONSHIP.

Date. Dance. Drink. Drive. Rage.

Everything is sudden and overwhelming.

One of my friends says '*Loneliness can be a curse. People go overboard with ANYTHING.*'

I ask- 'what things.' He says I may be subjected to peer-pressure. Right. Peer-pressure. Anything! Be it sex, boozing, drugs.

He says I may be subjected to peer-pressure.

Sure but peer-pressure is however often over-rated.

You can easily influence and can get influenced at the same time.

All depends upon the ratio of self-control.

...

Couples in love in the shady areas.

It's like witnessing the movie scenes live.

Cars going eco-friendly and cigarettes-the major source of pollution.

In school there's uniformed clothing, same shoes, no gadgets, and no open hang outs in the school premises.

Here in college you have no bars.

*Well, my family background doesn't allow me go overboard with anything. So, more or less, I'm going to assume the role of **Tiresias,** a sad spectator of the modern wasteland.'*

Yours

Vyom

*****

27

The Guilt Story

It is the second week of the college. Hauz Khas Village. Unlike other hot and misty days usually charring us to bones, the day is overcast. Planning a day long tour of this unique village, we set out early morning as it's a Sunday.

Let the word 'village' not confuse. It is an urban village! One can't expect to see the paddy fields, the mud huts or shepherds we usually come across in a village. The name is derived from the Urdu word 'Hauz' which means a water tank and 'Khas' which means special or to be precise- royal. This large water reservoir was built by Khilji to supply water to the inhabitants of Siri, the second medieval city of the Delhi Sultanate.

It's been after ages I feel I have visited such a serene place on a beautiful day like this. I take a leisurely stroll all by myself. Several other buildings like Mosque, Madrasa and Royal Tombs have been built overlooking the beautiful lake adding to the alluring features of the place.

'Lovely day isn't it?' one of my friends exclaims.

'I swear it is! Is this place always as quiet as the present moment?' I ask curiously wondering if this is going to be my best hideaway during my entire stay in the city.

'Let this quiet morning stretch to late afternoon! The place is going to be abuzz with activity AND with EVERYTHING you could ever imagine!' he chuckles.

'Really?'

'Yeah'

He's right. After a little while as we have had a refreshing walk along the reservoir, we wander down the crowded paths jostling with people. The shops are pretty small yet very attractive. A number of eateries catch our attention making us experience hitherto been evaded pangs of hunger.

'Let's have a cup of tea. What say?' I suggest.

'Not here Vyom. I'll take you to a real nice *chai* shop.'

'But...err...' I mumble.

'No worries man! It isn't an expensive place at all. I would've loved to take you to one but I know your theory of self-respect-n-all...knowing you wouldn't allow me to pay...I suggested *Thadi*.' Vihan opens up.

'Thanks *yaar*! You are a wonderful person.' I compliment.

'Believe me, I am not. I respect you as a person *yaar* otherwise making friends with a guy who totally abstains from all joys...' he condenses.

'Thanks. THANKS!'

Tucked atop a lovely terrace, *Thadi* offers a beautiful view of the calm lake and the lush greens that balm your stressed mind like anything!

This is a crowded place too with so many *murhaas* occupied by lovely-lively couples chatting over steaming hot glasses of chai.

Surrounded by such lush greenery, this is just the place to spend a day out.

Adjacent to the village is a sprawling park, the Deer Park, I'm told.

Here u can have rooms on rent @ a moderate price. It's one of the best hangout places for youngsters. Your ID is not checked here. Then there is *My Bar. S*urprisingly enough u cum across a no. of students boozing & smoking. Real nice food. No restrictions. Then there is this *Chaman-Lal Café cum Bar* where u can see alcohol flowing free. The best favourite bunking places...

'If you love the place so much, you can have a room on rent here. Rooms are pretty cheap here. I'm afraid though...' Vihan hesitates.

'*Vaise toh* I'm pretty satisfied with the room I'm presently sharing with other three guys...what's your proposal...*haan?*

'Nothing. The place doesn't suit you.'

'???'

A few guys and girls at some distance bursting out in a sudden bout of laughter catch my attention next. One stud, the tallest amongst them all, seems to be preparing a cigar. He empties a paper, collects some tobacco, nicotine, hash, weed etc. etc. as I gather from their talks, and rolls it. It is then lit and smoked by a few of them including girls.

'*Lemme* try once.' A pretty girl with pimpled cheeks asks for it.

It hits her at once, as it seems.

I'm stupefied.

'*Bhai maine kaha tha na. Yahi matlab tha mera. Yeh toh rojana ki cheejen hein inke liye. Tu chal yahan se. 'Lemme try once.' Yeh feeling hi marva deti hai saali.* Once you try, you experience a strange trip. And after one trip, you are supposed to stop. If you don't...you are an addict man!' says Vihan.

'Experienced *haan?* What made you fall into all this?' I ask.

'The easy access. *Aur kya?* Colleges *ke bahar khule aam bikti hein yeh sab cheejen.* It isn't directly easy but once you find out from which of the most unexpected sources you can procure these things, it is pretty easy. And then, there's no looking back man.' he sighs.

The group seems to have overheard us.

We leave the place.

We decide to sit by the lake.

'Do you regret?' I ask, trying to read his actual state of mind.

'I do. I regret this more than anything else Vyom.'

'???'

'...it was a Sunday night. Everything was planned amongst us. We were going to do something new the first time. We needed a girl for the purpose. They forced me. My friends. My girl-friend was to be the scape goat. She loved me so much, readily agreed to accompany me not knowing of course what she was in for. It was a common friend's birthday. This was what we had planned as a gift for him. He had turned eighteen, you know. A big zing-thing amongst us, as it goes. We were all so dizzyingly excited. A bunch of wretched fellows ...'

'Continue.'

'...we would gladly have enjoyed, boozed, smoked and the like... but his parents invited him home with all of us you know...we imagined it would be a dull party at his home with so many elders around...but we were wrong. His father had arranged all! Drinks flowing free...dance and *masti*...my girl-friend was with me all this while clinging to me in her own very sweet way...we took their leave late night...and reached the Disc...' Vihan stares me hard steering a steady course instead of wavering about in panic.

'Move on. I'm listening.'

'I'm a wretched person friend. I don't deserve to be with you.' Vihan begins to sob.

'Vihan! Tell me what happened next! It'd heal your wound! Trust me!'

'It was some powdered drug known as Forget Pill that we mixed in her drink.'

'Didn't she suspect...I mean...no change in the taste of her drink or *smthn* she might've...umm...doubted?'

'That's how the drug helps in sexual assaults. The drugs often have no colour, smell, or taste. So you can't tell if you are being drugged. When slipped into a drink, a dye in these new pills makes clear liquids turn bright blue and dark drinks turn cloudy. But this colour change might be hard to see in a dark drink like cola or dark beer, or in a dark room. The drugs can make you become weak and confused — so that you are unable to refuse sex or defend yourself.'

'Oh!'

'Within ten to fifteen minutes your senses begin to waver. It affects your memory part. The brain stops responding. If you are drugged, you might not even remember what actually happened while you were drugged. It's only after a stretch of a fixed time period...that you have your senses back...not able to recall however if there was some sexual acts committed by you... before you fell asleep.'

I'm shocked.

'...she was dancing in my arms...laughing...on the top of the world! And then...it acted very fast. Her voice began to slur. It looked like she was dreaming. Her heart rate went slower...we found the moment favourable and took her to a nearby lounge... she was perhaps aware of what was happening to her...around her...but unable to move...her perception went distorted...it was a gang rape...I hate myself...oh! How I hate myself!' sobbing gets harder.

A few people stare us suspiciously.

We let go.

'She must have severed all her emotional ties with you. *Nahin?*' I ask, my eyes stabbing him.

'Please don't look at me like this Vyom. I can't stand my own eyes in the mirror...had she known what had exactly happened... severed her ties with me, slapped me hard...quarrelled with me...I wouldn't feel that guilty, you know...

...it was a total black out...she recalled nothing! She woke up in her own couch...messaged me 'a good morning' like she did everyday...asked for a meeting to thank me for the beautiful party the previous night...she just complained of some breathing trouble as she woke up...certain numbness...

...it was *Rohypnol* or *Ketamine*...I don't exactly remember the name for we had a discussed a number of them before hatching the cruel scheme on the innocent girl...she can't ever conceive now...she doesn't know that too of course...'

'OMG! I don't believe this! You could do all this! How could you?' he meets my frowning gaze.

'How the hell did she manage to reach home?' I ask.

The ensuing silence is tense.

'I dressed her up, lifted her in my arms, put her in my car and dropped her home after we had had too much of her...'sighs and sobs.

His throat moves up and down as if he is trying to swallow a boulder.

The big unseen hammer of tension begins beating beneath my skin.

'Did you meet her?'

'How could I?' he is hardly audible; is unable to talk to me eye to eye.

'Don't ever do that! You scoundrel! I hate you!' I slap him HARD.

He doesn't react for the moment. He hides his face against his knees, flinches and cries out, throwing his arms.

I can't stand his company anymore.

But I can't leave him with devil-may-care approach.

I care.

I do care.

*****

28

Magnetism Works Here

Dating happens to be the favourite pass-time. If it's a girl proposing a guy for a date, the place is, no doubt, *Connaught Place* where she shops 2 her heart's content n u r digging ur purse for every lil' damn thing her feminine heart catches a fancy for. Or u can go 2 movies wid her, a routine thing for college-going ones.

Flaunting ur blossoming figure is the sole purpose behind all dressing patterns.

~~Bhayia n Didi~~ -not allowed.

(Considered derogatory terms.)

Inside the campus- it is a no smoking zone. But right outside the campus there are as many stalls for cigarettes as one can imagine. A pretty good number of brands available. A youth can consume easily two packs of cigarettes a day.

AND why should boys have all the fun?

...

Inside the college canteen there's only vegetarian food available. But right outside the campus non-veg food stalls do good business in-fact.

There are all kinds of students. The dumb lot. The intellectual lot. Magnetism works here. You'll find your kind of lot to be mixed with, pretty soon. May be the first day itself. Girls prefer the first one (the dumb lot) as they commonly own pretty big cars and other accessories.

Vihan gets 25000/-per month from his Dad for his personal expenses which is obviously apart from the accommodation, stationary, and fee which they pay for him. The diet is completely ignored by him. He prefers fine dining at expensive restaurants than in the college canteen as others usually do. He'll go anywhere, anytime with his backpack! His is a wandering soul, kind of. He vibes with all kinds of girls very well; makes them feel *very special* in his own way.

While I live frugally and don't dream to own a fancy car or apartment, he is cut out to dream big. Even that 25000/- doesn't last for the entire month so he pays a secret visit to his Mom who lives in a high-class flat with her dream man. Not of course her husband. She's recently bought him an electric blue car which he really-really loves and he plans to love it even when one day he buys his own BMW.

As far as I'm concerned, my college fee and other necessary expenses have already taken a financial toll and my Dad will continue to work hard for how many years more...I don't know... to pay off the debts he has incurred for my admission here.

I have been preparing for UPSC exam side by side.

I need to work hard.

But as long as I'm here, I can't live in isolation.

So I have made some friends.

But I always know my limits.

'You know what, Vyom? My Dad is soon gonna buy the coolest car ever!' exclaims Vihan.

'Which one?' I'm intrigued.

'None other than BMW 6 Series coupé!'

'Wow! Great man!' Sahil congratulates him, a sober guy with soberer tastes as compared to Vihan.

'Hey Sahil! *Tu bhi toh maaldaar baap ka beta hai yaar!* Which car do you have man?' asks Vihan, pretty excited.

'None yet.' answers Sahil in a very cool manner.

'*Kya baat kar raha hai?* You have no cars at home? I mean no cars actually?'

'We have. But none belongs to me yet.' smiles Sahil.

'Oh C'mon! What's the difference?'

'*Tu nahin samjhega.*' Sahil beams with a queer sense of satisfaction.

He's going to be a self-made man.

A brand new BMW whizzes past them.

'I love the car man! We'll go for the same colour if my Dad agrees.' brags Vihan.

The car takes a smooth U turn and stops at the college gate.

'I'm awfully sorry Sir! You'll have to drive home today. My wife is going to be discharged from the hospital today.' the driver modestly places the car's keys in Sahil's fist. He also gives a sweets' pack to him.

'I'm happy for you. A boy or a girl?' beams Sahil.

'Boy!' the driver warmly responds.

'*Mubarak ho!* Take care. I'll manage.' Sahil smiles back.

'*Kya saale...!!??!! Mmm...*' Vihan open his mouth.

Sahil thrusts a *laddoo* in Vihan's mouth before he's done with his usual ooooooos and ohhhhhhhs.

*****

29

It's Okay if You Don't Love Me

There are many courses available here in the college.

After one passes class twelfth, the most probable answer to the question, '*What course do you intend to opt for?*' is-'*Well, I'm not so sure still. Let's see. If I'm able to secure a place in DU...I will have done well...can pick up any course...otherwise...let's see...*'

Girls generally prefer BJMC i.e. Bachelor in Journalism and Mass Communication. There are other combinations available like BA+ LL.B., B.COM + LL.B., B.B.A+LL.B. and many more.

To be a C.A. has been much opted for an option especially amongst boys. No more a popular course though as far as my calculation goes.

Moreover there's so much stress on pursuing a passion these days. You may come across the most weird girls and guys during your hostel life and the tragedy is that you have to t.o.l.e.r.a.t.e...

The YouTube guitar man- he will have an instrument at all times. It will probably be a guitar or, God help us all, a bamboo flute. You will find him in the common room, your room, dining room and bathroom. The cringe-inducing, emotional close-eyed singing face. Nothing is more uncomfortable than when a total stranger's underlying emotion surfaces through song. He will pester you whole night to watch guitar videos on YouTube.

Then there is this **mobile addict**-'*It was horrible, Dad, everything in the canteen was deep-fried.*' With no regard whatsoever for anyone else in the room, he/she will yap and dramatically coo to his/her loved ones over the phone, describing everything from his/her breakfast to his/her bowel movements. He/ she will keep you up all night. The bags under your eyes will perhaps give you the wandering looks of a drug dealer but...you can't really escape.

The clingers- will find any reason, any reason at all, to break the ice and never let it melt. You can't escape the clingers. Once they've got you talking, they will never leave your side. They assume you'll give them company at everything be it- cooking, sightseeing, laundering or anything!

Then there are **Snobs**, the **Social Hygienists**, etc. etc. You may laugh away the disturbance caused by this friend of yours who dines on only the most pungent and noisily packaged foodstuffs... at all times.

How many times though?

...

The campus is so huge that you are very likely to get lost unless you carry the college map in hand.

The security system in the college is very tight. You can be allowed inside the campus only if you carry your scholar I Card.

The day- scholars can stay in the premises till eight in the evening.

There are a number of gates leading to the campus. There're guards at each of the gates. You aren't allowed to bring an outsider into the college premises just to *show off* you know.

Within a month or so however, if you have the guts you know, you learn all the tricks to fly in the teeth of so called rules. You can bribe the gate keepers telling them plainly that you forgot to bring the identity card.

This happens twenty-two-days-a-month you know, common problem with all. ☺

Even the gatekeepers have to survive, no? ;)

There are lectures organized in the grand auditoriums. No body's interested to listen anything. They are too much in love with their up-to-the-minute mobiles- n-all to pay heed to the stale lectures. There are however jammers all around the place. The network strength fails almost as they enter the auditoriums.

The attendance will be taken right here after the lecture so...no escape.

...

Presently the lecture has been organized for the fresher ones especially to give them an approach against the foreseen ragging and the like. After the lecture there will be a question-answer session. Scholars enjoy this concluding part; ask the *stttupidest* questions just to embarrass the lecturers.

There are official fresher parties.

There are unofficial fresher parties too where drugs and drinks are served in open.

Most of the guys are chain smokers. Hardly 10% of the money they get from home is spent on studies and ambitions.

...

Well...

The preparations for one more event are in full swing. *The Fresh Face*. The Fresh Face can also be known as *The Delhi Face*. It will be published in Delhi newspaper. An entire page dedicated to you, your personality, your dreams, your whims, your likes and dislikes, your routine etc. etc.

A BIG THING you know.

The event is to be organized in the college itself. You can see a crowd of scholars full of beans. Even lecturers seem to be pretty keyed up about the whole affair. A scholar is ready to do anything...anything...to be The Fresh Face. It is big temptation. You may be asked to dance before all in the open premises or sing maybe or even self-abuse!

You have to undergo whatever humiliation heaped upon you IF you wanna be...

...

...

New pairings go on amongst hostellers. There are many brothels on G.B.Road which is commonly known as Red Light Area. They are completely organized societies. Sex is legalized here. There are all types of girls-the regular ones and the high standard ones. Charges vary from girl to girl depending upon her figure and face; also vary from guy to guy depending upon his status.

These brothels are raided too often by Police. It is just a formality though because people into this business have got too thick skinned to bother about such things.

Vihan tells, some girls studying in the high class colleges don't mind accompanying a group of guys to Goa or any other fancy place of their choice, having drinks and fun in cars on the way or even getting registered as their lawfully wedded wives in grand hotels. Of course they need to remember that they're supposed to put on a piece of ornament be it *Mangalsutra* or a gold ring that might be established as an engagement ring.

A girl might surprise you by telling that she wouldn't be picked up by *you* or go with *you* where *you* want to take her; rather *she* would pick you up in *her* own car and take you to a place of *her* choice, be it her own separate flat or a hotel!

Business you know.

There's a price list for everything.

Charges differ according to your requirement- you wanna kiss her, cuddle her, talk to her or have sex with her.

There are no regrets.

Sex is no more a taboo to recoil from.

Girls take pride while sharing their previous night experiences. They rather blow their own horn.

...

'You know what?'

'!!!!!'

'I slept with a tycoon last night!'

'Don't tell me!'

'Yesss!'

'How did you manage to trap him?'

'Facebook Page my darlings!'

'He contacted you or you hunted him?'

'He did!'

'*Khoool yaar!* You must have extracted a handsome amount?'

'*Aur nahin toh kisliye? Kharcha toh nikalna padta hai na yaar!*'

'Party tonight?'

'Not tonight dearie. Right now I'm going back to my room and stretch my limbs. Couldn't sleep a wink the whole night.'

'Had fun?'

'Of course! He was so driven and passionate!'

'He came out of the blue and made you a fat cat in just one night!'

'He belongs to Mauritius! Was here for some official meeting, I guess.'

'Next?'

'Nothing. He wants me to pose the same fire ball on the couch the next week as he comes. Gosh! He is brutally demanding!' she answers, her sexy mouth rendered sexier by the gold nose ring hovering over it.

'Ooooh!!! We are having goose bumps you know!'

'Given that life is so short and fragile, surely each of us should be trying to extract the most out of every breath, every fleeting moment.'

'What was the size?' one asks, her super huge chandelier earrings dancing with stolen pleasure.

'Shut up!' they all giggle.

145

"Highbury bore me. Richmond and Kew
Undid me. By Richmond I raised my knees
Supine on the floor of a narrow canoe."

"My feet are at Moorgate, and my heart
Under my feet. After the event
He wept. He promised a 'new start.'
The broken fingernails of dirty hands."

(Wasteland)

*****

30

Feeding on Reminiscences

Exams' pressure is closing on in. Trisha's room-mates have gone to the library to prepare notes. It's only when the sword of exams hangs over their heads, they plan to do some studies, the serious kind. Trisha doesn't feel like. She confines herself to the room and is presently pacing to and fro in the small terrace attached. She can behold, as far as her sight goes, girls sitting in pairs in the lawn with books in hands.

She had nursed the thought that the hostel life would provide her the much needed change. Now she realizes that the grass isn't any greener over here too. She is fed up of the girls' school. It might be a dream for a guy to be around a huge crowd of Double X chromosomes but being a girl yourself, it can be no less than a nightmare.

There in the old school, being surrounded by boys was so much fun. It always motivated you to be a live wire. Here you can't carry fake brands without being caught. Using make-up gets strengthened manifold but good looks don't get you anywhere. Since every male professor teaches hundreds of girls, you actually have to study hard and score well.

The great feminist writers and singers become your role models. Without even realizing yourself, you become, in the due course of time, a hard core feminist. Here is where you realize that 'Mean Girls' isn't just a movie. The same crazy shit goes on every moment.

Trisha is weepy today.

She is missing her Dad, missing the selfless service her Mom gave, missing her dance sessions with Mom loaded with fun, missing the school where she would be messing about most of the times, and...missing Amish too.

...

What lovely moments were those! How, at first had he brushed his lips soaked in desire against her virgin lips; how the two had made love in the ten-by-ten bedroom of his, panting, moaning and going wilder each moment; how at last she lay motionless for long in his arms completely naked against him. The first time ever!

She has hormonal stirrings for him, she guesses.

So many twitchy days and agonizing nights have kicked off the calendar since the day.

He hasn't tried even a single time to talk to her, connect to her in any way.

He really didn't love her like she did.

Wait wait...!

Did...she...r.e.a.l.l.l.y.l.o.v.e.?

R.e.a.l.l.y...?

Perhaps...yes. Perhaps not.

It is just possible that *she* used *him* to experience the zing thing.

Wait wait...

What if she had really got pregnant?

Well, she would have been screwed.

Worry pulses inside her like some creepy crawling thing!

Better to be born as a guy, she thinks. No parental pressure, no pressure to fit in the commonly acceptable zero figure, no judging eyes all the time, no menstrual cramps, no pills, no pregnancies, no abortions.

'*Why should boys have all the fun?*' she visualizes Priyanka Chopra's current advertisement.

'*Why should I be tied down by unwritten rules?*' she recalls a question asked by whom, she fails to recall.

A few more lines come floating in her mind...that's the problem with her. She reads, absorbs subconsciously but can't really trace the roots when she needs.

'*Life is short;*

So break the rules,

Forgive quickly,

Kiss slowly,

Love truly,

Laugh uncontrollably,

& never regret anything that made you smile.'

'He did make me smile but...

I can't really forgive him.' she mumbles.

*****

31

Love You Tia!

Vyom is home.

'I'm proud of you my son! You have finally cracked the exam you have been trying hard for. Now we are not far from our dreams. Money cushions things son. Nothing has been hidden from you. You have seen me working for overtimes and how I have invited untimely old age upon myself working, working and working more.' the father shifts his tongue insides his cheeks perhaps too overcome by this good news to express his joy. His eyes swim in tears.

'I'll never let you down Dad.' Vyom manages to make his way in the warm embrace of his father. It's like a hot flood of emotions inside him, scorching its way through his veins.

'I'm sure you never will. Go and take blessings from your Mom. Thank God! She's just fine. Go. She is in the kitchen cooking food for you. Aah! It's the day we have long been waiting for.' Dad heaves a sigh of relief.

'*Aa jao, mein kitchen mein hi hun.*' she calls out. Seems like she's been overhearing the conversation.

'Don't tire yourself Maa. I'll cook.'

'I'm absolutely fine *beta*. You have made me proud! All those days you had not even slept well. I was crestfallen...a.n.d...I thought I would never be well again. I thought I had better die thinking of the swollen figures my surgery and medicines might incur. But neither of you two surrendered. You served me night and day...' a guilty shiver.

'We did because we love you Mom! We are family!'

'*Arrey bhai* ! How long to wait for the sweets you made?' interrupts Vyom's father.

…

…

A little later…

Vyom is in his room. He can't speak for surety if he is happy. Of course he is feeling good for his parents but what about his happiness?

Can he ever be happy without Tia?

He is commuting on a stream of thoughts.

It is just possible she might have hitched with someone else.

After all she had everything a guy might ask for.

Perhaps he didn't deserve her.

'Missing you' he mutters lowly under the breath.

Her memories are looming around.

How long…how long would he be able to escape?

He feels smothered within as if a hand locked around his neck.

He reads the long cherished letter again.

The words hang in the air like swinging swords.

…

'Dear Vyom,

It's my very first letter to you…to any guy in this lifetime of mine. I *dunno* how to. I've often noticed that '*smthn*' in your eyes which perhaps goes *arnd* by the name of '*luv*' or *y wud u* always cum out of the blue as if, whenever I be in some trouble? …

…you've been taking care of me like a loyal friend…a silent friend though. I can't however remain mute any longer for I'm overawed u know…and must name this caring and sharing…

151

...I know I may not be the right choice for your kind of a guy...I know I'm not that '*karwa chauth*' kind of ritualistic gal who'd serve your parents with the same devotion as you do. Till date I have been a carefree girl...you know...living for the moment and letting the wind take me where it will...but I...I think I'm changing you know! ...I...I am nothing but a sickly plant that keeps sulking unless you cast it a look...and...and it perks up at once if you do! What do you call it? I choose to call it love...Stop caring for me if you don't love...Can't say '*forever yours or smthn like that*' until you choose to...'

...

...

Vyom, for the first time sits to write a letter- a love letter. He can't really decide if he should...or if there be any possibility to have her back in his life.

He can't concentrate, stretches languorously and thinks hard.

Late morning stretches to late afternoon and then into the fading light.

A number of friends have been home to congratulate him but he didn't mention her name to them though knowing he could get to know where she was.

'Dear Tia

I have been feeding long on nostalgia. I'm missing you! It's not like I never loved you. I loved you from the depth of my heart. Your voice still rings in my ears assuming thousands lovely tones...

Since childhood, my parents tell, I have been a responsible child never demanding things like kids generally would...may be because I knew it wasn't that easy for my parents to fulfil those. They couldn't get me admitted to a good private school until when it was pretty late. It was good in one respect though- *I always knew my limitations*. I couldn't afford what you guys could. I couldn't go to the club, to the excursions that might cost my parents hell...naturally you took it as indifference on my part...arrogance may be...actually...I couldn't ever think of being arrogant for I was the lowest privileged teen in the class...I couldn't fluently talk in English like you did...so one more reason I never mingled up...was...I suffered from low-esteem.

But I knew my targets.

I had to grab them.

I couldn't pursue my ambitions if I indulged in any scandalous behaviour or got trapped in the so called love-traps.

It's not that I didn't understand what extra amount of attention you paid me from the day one. Frankly admitting though...I took your gestures to be the fancies of a girl who belonged to a well-heeled family...one who could get anything she put her finger on...I was keeping up appearances...though loving you deep enough...believe me dear...it was an oppressive silence. I know I have hurt you. No fine word or phrase would make any sense... still...let me say...for I have silently conversed with you for hours at a stretch...giving my reasons for overlooking you...I heard you had slashed your wrist after we had talked the last time...your wrist...and my heart...was awash with blood.

I could've followed my instincts and rushed to your arms...but... this 'but' has never stopped chasing me...a strong desire to live... to live with you by my side forever, has too often surfaced... but I have determinedly pushed it away...coz...to me...love only existed in my delirium...with a gritted heart, I threw myself into my studies...but today I'm wide awake. The invisible cord between us has never broken. I love you Tia! It hasn't been a linking of the flesh for you know I have never ever...I'm unable to hold back my emotions any longer. The fantasies we had secretly built up are on their way to materialise. You know what? I have cracked the exam with flying colours...need you by my side to celebrate.

Without you... even success means nothing...

I'm nothing but a heap of rubble without you.'

All yours

Vyom

...

Vyom slightly trembles.

Back in bed, he melts into low, timid, suppressive sobs till his breath steadies and deepens.

What if she didn't need him any longer?

What if her love really was just the fancy of a teenage heart?

Disappointment presses on his chest like a slab of concrete.

For the first time...he allows the waves of tears and supressed longings their natural expression.

*****

32

Crying for the Lost Moon

Vyom has always been an early bird. He wakes up even earlier than usual today and moves out for a jog. His heart gives a tremendous leap as his eyes follow a flight of birds etched black against the orange haze strewn around, screeching past him.

His eyes chase them for long in fearful fascination.

He doesn't feel like jogging after a quarter of an hour or so.

He can't concentrate; sits on a bench in the park.

Drops of precipitation glisten on his forehead.

With the placid rays of the sun falling on his face, his complexion changes from mud brown to a glowing toffee.

...his love...his is the love of the soul.

He doesn't surely lust after Tia like the game went on in DU.

Allowing his breathlessness to subside, he finally dials her number.

And the same loved fruity voice it is!

'Hello. May I know who is calling?'

'Err...it's me.' Vyom's expressions go sour fearing something.

'Me? Who me?' against all odds, could this be him, Tia asks within.

'It's me. Vyom.' Vyom fabricates a fake smile looking around.

There are kids playing Frisbee.

'*Whaaat? Reallllly???*' Tia wipes away the messengers of joy that dance in her eyes.

'Hmm...m.' he wipes away the drops of an unseen pain lurking in his eyes.

'I don't believe this! When did you get back?'

'A day ago.'

'A day? A day you said! That means a full twenty four HOURS! That means...leave it...u know my Maths...but if I had been at your place...leave that too. You won't understand.'

'*Bolo naa!*'

'No use Vyom. No use.'

'I wanted to! Believe me but then...I thought...perhaps...'

'That's what I mean. You've changed a lot. Never mind though. I have changed too.'

'Can I see you?'

'I'm afraid, no.'

'The ground for denial?'

'*Ektuallllly*...mmm...'

'I understand.' Vyom lets out a sigh of submission.

'I mean I don't want to hurt you. I *can* but I *would* not. I *should* not rather.'

Silence.

Painful on both ends.

'U there?' asks Tia.

'Ummm...yes...well, it's okay. I just wanted to...fine F.I.N.E. No problem.' Vyom forces his lips to smile at the little boy who's come close to the bench to fetch the Frisbee.

'You wouldn't ask the reason?' asks Tia.

'You may tell if u want. M listening.'

The moist in his eyes seems to have washed out all the colours from the park.

'V.y.o.m...I still remember your words, even the way you intoned them. I was shattered you know. The faint shadow of protection I always clung to, had suddenly disappeared. Didn't know what to do without you. I was lost...'

Vyom can feel her voice going shaky.

'But then...I never promised. Did I...ever?' asks Vyom.

'No. You didn't. I was a fool you know.'

The threads of feelings on both ends are going sharp and tingling, pricking their way through their veins.

'I love you Tia.'

Birds cheerfully toot, twit and twitter.

No answer.

She would have danced with joy but...

'It's too late Vyom.' Tia pretends the same dejected tone while actually rushing to throw open the doors and windows of her room.

She lets light and air seep into her.

She lets the room breathe.

...

The colossal canvas of his dreams fails to stir any emotions in her, as it seems.

...

'I'm committed to someone else now.' Tia suppresses the stockpile of giggles that stands impatient on her lips to burst open.

'Ahh! I'm sorry. I...m really s.o.r.r.y. Take care. Bi.'

'I'm sorry for you Vyom but...'

'I understand...my mistake. Why you be sorry?'

Vyom flashes a fake smile towards the skies and walks away.

*****

33

Tia Riding on the Wings of Joy

'*Mommy!!!*'

'What happened darling?'

'La.la.la.la.la.la.' Tia is dancing with a teddy in arms.

'Looks like the moon has fallen in your hands. Hey! What's it?'

'M.o.r.e. .t.h.a.n. t.h.a.t. la.la.la...'

Her Mom takes the teddy from her daughter's hands and hurls it softly onto the bed.

'May I?' Tia's Mom offers her hand for dance.

'*Umm hum!*' Tia quivers with joy.

'I love you Tia!' her Mom plays Vyom.

'*Mein toh jane kabse...*' a beautiful pink colour surges through her throat finally settling on her succulent cheeks.

'Hee hee. So when did it happen?' asks her Mom fondly.

'Just now. Just now.' Tia is riding on the wings of joy.

'So he finally realized...'

'Yesss *maa!* You know what? I said-'It's too late Vyom.' Tia assumes a made up tone tinged with pain.

'Then then?' her mother asks, excited.

'Then what? Then he was like- *I. u.n.d.e.r.s.t.a.n.d. It's all my doing. Why you be sorry?*' Tia doubles with laughter.

'*My doll!*' Mom takes daughter in a warm embrace.

'I waited patiently because I knew this would be so one day.' Tia rests her head on her mother's shoulders crying out of joy.

'You deserved. You've changed yourself so entire for the sake of his love!'

'You happy *naa* maa?'

'I'm happy darling! Why wouldn't I be? He is such a nice guy. I'll ask your dad that we visit his parents very soon.'

'Mom!'

'Hmmm?'

'Love you!'

'Love you too honey!'

'If you had not...saved me Maa, I wouldn't have seen the day.' Tia goes mum.

'Oh! Let's not. Let's not talk of the day. It gives me creeps.'

'If I could do it all again...! I wish I never would've made the scars on my wrists. I can't explain how much I was hurt by the rejection...by his going away... so much so that I chose to end my life. Luckily, I'm still alive. Thank you Mom! But for you...I wouldn't have seen this beautiful day.'

*****

34

I Need Your Love

There is always someone who wants to be the next Kate or Naomi, but despite what the movies tell us, becoming a model isn't just about being tall and beautiful. It's about having the uniqueness, talent and drive to back up those looks. Telling your parents that you are interested in modelling is a big task itself. If they object then jus' leave it there or who will be funding things? If they think it sounds good, start working towards it. You may star in pageants, go for training to studios or delve right into the modelling world.

Failures will be there no doubt but then all you need to remember is that great models have also begun when they are teens like you.

The magazine photo shoots, commercials, catwalk for labels, swimsuit or catalogue modelling- Aliya has been figuring out all these things for long. She's been sitting for endless hours online searching for modelling agencies. A simple 'model agency' query garners a lot of results. Not knowing there are plenty of scammers out there to take advantage of an aspiring model, she's agreed to pay money upfront at times. She's been filling a number of online forms, sending her photos and stats. She has also gone online to Craigslist and Model Mayhem and such other sites to find a photographer that is looking to build a portfolio. This is what we call T.F.P. modelling. Time for Prints. Here you exchange your time in return for photographs for your portfolio.

She's spent a lot to get professional shoots done and yet it's not the first time she is told she is not the one the agency is looking for.

'I understand Aliya.' consoles Rohan, grabbing her hand.

'*Mera dil kahta hai* Aliya...you'll get signed soon.'

'I'm getting sick of all this I tell you!' she takes his hand with a sigh of helplessness.

'Your ambition has taken you away from home. Now you must make the best out of the worst. Rejections are pretty natural baby, in the beginning. It happens.' says Rohan.

'I know that Rohan. What I'm worried about is that my cash is running out. I think I need a back-up plan.'

'Perhaps yes. You do. But if you manage somehow there's a world of opportunities out there. Models like Kate Moss and others have transformed their grand looks into lucrative careers with their smart brains. *Tu bhi ek din...dekh lena...mein bol raha hun naa?'* Rohan tries to cheer her up.

'These modelling classes are costing me a hell! I feel sick at times of people telling me about the significance of a *signature walk* and all that. Instructions like *'shoulders back and relaxed', 'hips out and forward', 'legs straight'*, and *'one foot in front of the other'* sounded interesting at first but...hey c'mon! Will someone tell me when the hell am I going to be a model? I have been open to all suggestions that come my way still some sound too rude like *'Remember not to bounce or sway your hips too much!'* I'm supposed to take tips they give as per their need based on their clothing designs contemporary or more outlandish.' she grudges.

'Take it as constructive criticism. This will eventually help you to unleash your inner model. I know it is an expensive affair babe. But it can be worth it in the long run. All you need is a little patience and an added boost of confidence.'

'But for you by my side, I might've given up long back.' Aliya kisses his hand.

'Awww! C'mon! I'm always there with my babe. I'll do my best to facilitate your career.' Unlike Sarah, Aliya loves to be called a babe and cuddled like one.

'And what about yours?'

'Mine what?'

'Career. *Buddhu!* What else?'

'Well Aliya, I feel so insecure. I wonder if I would ever be able to find my feet.'

'Why wouldn't you? If I can, then you can!'

'Now c'mon please! Stop behaving like my Mom...' Rohan giggles.

'...and start behaving like what?' Aliya glows with a smile, a delicate sylph like creature in a polka dotted top and small pony tail.

'My girlfriend.' he gestures her to come to his arms; shedding his broken bird image.

She hides in his arms trying to forget her frustrations for the time being and have some good time.

They have been meeting at Anurag's place time and again.

'Can't live without you.' Rohan gets sentimental, kisses her madly all over her face.

'Love you too boy.' she responds with the same warmth.

'Take this off.' Rohan hisses a loving command.

'First you go and lock the door.' she hisses back.

Rohan closes the door and brings down the curtains on the crowded road. Aliya looks very pretty in the scattering of beams falling from the moon through the window curtains. The two are on the bed soon, her hair splayed out all over the pillow. Her lips are painted in Cupid's bow. Rohan shuts her lip glossed giggles with a full kiss.

It's all dark almost and mossy outside. It looks like it's going to rain. The giant heart called Gurgaon huffs and puffs outside. The fact that it is raining outside can't stop the tumultuous hustle and bustle on the roads.

He blows soft breaths on her hair. She turns towards him as instinctively as a flower to the sun. Today she is in blues more than ever. So she requires these delicate touches more than ever.

Mood swings.

One moment she hates his sweaty smell clinging to her being; the other moment she dotes on him.

'Love you more than anything else babe.' Rohan squeezes her in his arms and enjoys the sight when she lets out a small yelp of pain.

Their voices are soft and husky. Next she pulls him close to her mouth and the two experiences a full kiss again. The two make love. They roll off the bed on the cold floor and there are more of yelps, sighs, huffs-n-puffs and tears lurking at their eyelids due to the intense joy-n-satisfaction.

'Sometimes I get the vibe that...'

'What?' asks Rohan enjoying the feel of proximity within. Finally the patient wait has brought the two closer.

'That it's a temporary phase...I mean...will you always be there with me?' Aliya blinks back tears.

'For sure *Babu!*' he caresses her hair.

Their heartbeats quicken as they hear the shuffle at the steps.

No door-bell rang that means they didn't even realize all this while that there was no electricity while...

'OMG! Anurag!' Aliya utters with a toss of her pony tail, rushing to collect her clothes.

'No need to panic. He knows everything, no?' Rohan comforts her picking up the pair of jeans and the T- shirt from the tangled heap of their clothes on the floor.

'Still...it's embarrassing.' she looks sad, very sad as if a raw nerve touched again.

'Tomorrow? Noon time?' Rohan seeks a promise for the next day meeting.

'Nope! I have a call. Will meet for sure if I'm selected. We'll celebrate then.'

Rohan opens the door.

Anurag looks drunk and is with a girl lisping around him.

'Ho-hai!' Anurag throws a quick glance at Aliya's face.

The lean dimples flash and are suppressed immediately.

*****

35

Just One Pill, Not a Big Deal

Hi diary,

Mentioning no time for there isn't any time awareness left in my mind anymore. What all I find around me is total dark...be it day or night. Didn't feel like writing for long. Sorry for this absence.

It was the worst day of my life perhaps...

The more I try to climb up the terrible hole I have dug myself into, the more I hit rock bottom. My big terror of course isn't that my parents would be reported of the theft I've made and been caught red handed but...that...now onwards I wouldn't be able to do it and m sure I *wud b* found dead *smwhr smdey*...

...I had bunked the classes today and been hanging around with friends the entire noon...the whole day is a blur as if...for all I'm able to recall is that I was drugged-up and didn't *really* know *wht was happenin'*...*or whr I was goin*...its...it's a total mess in my mind. I hv been goin 2 school late evrydey, takin Ecstasy, Cannabis, and other drugs n I've basically lost interest in evrythn...I know I'm on a slippery slope, downhill and fast...I'm worried sick, I'm grey and thin, my skin is appalling, doesn't glow anymo...I'm on a very short fuse the whole time...I remember the first day I came to the hostel...they gave me the key and I was like...what next!!! I sat the entire night on the floor, crying, making sense out of what I'd recently been through...life in this hostel is tedious and full of restrictions...m allowed to go out only two nights a week...of course I've been taking drugs from the day one I came here...but it'd have been all so different if I were home...I'm always waiting for money to arrive from Dad so that I could work out how many drugs I can afford to buy...

Mom is different, u know, brings me lot of food, doesn't give money at all...I feel like...like m a beggar dammit!!! Where to get the money from? A big question. So...I have been looking at everythn in d hostel, thinkin if I cud...can't go on like this...it's not life dammit!!!

M down n depressed the whole time and I...I miss my frens, my class, my Mom n Dad...wishing I cud get out of this rut...

Today I tried to steal cash and valuables propped up by my roommates from room no....shit! I'm forgetting the number...n the girl, Ananya, yeah the same who sleeps in nothing but her narrow bottomed BWitch Navy Blue panties...went straight towards the office and brought them for the live show...bloody girl...just bcoz...bcoz I had not shared my favourite lipstick with her the previous night!!!

Oh diary! I feel so very lonely at times. I regret being so lonely all through the ending up of my school years and not being able to change no matter how much I try. I regret turning to self-harm and drugs to fill the empty space around me.

I'm still feeling weaker after the day when I had slashed my wrist in a mood of self-pity you know. I couldn't just help it! It gave me queer sense of fulfilment! My room-mates had saved me by getting me hospitalized in time. The warden has been so very strict with me and so very watchful of my moves. That was the last warning I had from these authority people. No more am I going to be pardoned I know.

Mom n Dad will be arriving tomorrow. I wish I could kill myself before they find out I stole...! I'm so sorry Mom! I'm so sorry. I regret hurting you by hurting myself. I never wanted you to find out my love letters to Amish, the poems, the diary entries. I didn't want anyone inside my head, no matter how much I wanted the pain to stop. I was scared. So scared *Maa*! I was scared how would you guys feel when I told I was pregnant? It was pretty later that I came to know I wasn't! I didn't mean for you to find out things that way, and I'm sorry.

Violence was not the answer...both of us knew that...but...you slapped me!

Neither of us will ever get a chance to rewind and take back those physical and mental fights...you calmed down after a few days when your pain subsided a bit...you wanted me to know that we could take a deep breath and look forward...more than anything you were there for me, you assured. I remember the very words Mom-'*daughters rely on their mother the most but it's perfectly okay for the mother at times to rely on the daughter the same way.*' I remember you said...

But...dunno why still I felt I was alone in my struggles...and struggles for what, for God's sake? Dunno...may be the wish to be well liked in school and amongst friends, to be desired by some guy, to be pampered by you and Dad...to be famous, not to be compared with any child wonder kind AND not to be humiliated when I scored less than expected and so on...

I remember to have gone to a rave party with friends during my very first week in this hostel...it was maddening you know...I hadn't experienced such things in my home town ever...we would often do mischiefs at school, hook around, flirt, bunk classes and so on...well that's what we thought students' crazy world comprised of...here it is much more Mom...the guys urged me to try out just one pill saying- '*one small pill wouldn't be a big deal.*' After a little reluctance, I agreed. We were partying on and on! I was feeling extremely high!

I noticed they were all fine. I mean no problems. I didn't get hurt by the pill so I thought I could have it again you know kinda...I had an over dose. Five six pills plus something sticky. Crystalline. They called it Marijuana...

I hesitated not becoz...becoz I wanted to fly higher...my sense of perception was going weaker. My senses began wavering. At once...all at once I began feeling depressed like hell...I passed out! There! So humiliating! And...and I couldn't really manage on my own...they were all laughing. I was crumpled in a heap ashamed, couldn't stand without help...the help did come. One of the guards came in and kicked me out! I remember not how long did I keep lying there in the same condition. OMG!OMG!

I know Mommy, you haven't still forgiven me for having posted those dirty things on FB as how I felt about the guy n all...I couldn't just help it when I saw his latest pic with his wife on Instagram as if...as if nothing had happened between him and me!!! I was freaking out Mom! If I were happy in the relationship, I wouldn't be running to social media to share everything with all...like...like in my friends' cases...if they get a special bouquet from their crush or anything super sweet done to them, it would be known to everyone on Facebook and Twitter in just ten minutes!' sobs hard.

'I suffer from self -loathing Dad! Yesss. I hate myself!' pulls her hair in despair.

'Drugs lift my mood, relax me, even energize me...but I feel so low when I'm sober again...

...oh! Some body talk to me! I feel like sticking my head in the oven!'

...

...

Trisha looks at the clock.

It is 2 a.m.

Both Ananya and Navya are in the adjacent room on the pretext of group studies.

She knows the reason.

She has had a very bad fight with both.

They don't want to mess with her anymore.

Nor can Trisha bear anybody's presence in the room in a mental state like this.

Perhaps she will be taken back home today itself.

She starts packing things up desperately.

She is grimly trying to focus on what she's doing.

Fails to.

She wants to head out of this place even before the crack of dawn.

Unable to think any more, *anything*, she lets herself fall on the top of the bedspread.

She cries her heart out.

She looks like carrying the sorrow of the world on her shoulders.

36

The Wistful Longings

Vyom feels all emptied within.

He seems to have failed to fall in step with time.

Nothing matters now anyways.

His usually enthusiastic features are replaced with a deathly sombreness today. The creative spark that usually shines on his face is lost.

Sworn to secrecy earlier, he decides to talk to his Dad.

...

His dad is sitting on the front porch swing with a magazine in hand.

'Come-come-come! Sit.' His dad pats the space next to him.

'Well, you look sullen! U okay?'

'Dad!' Vyom's imploring eyes speak more than his tongue can.

'Bolo bhai kya hua! Sab theek toh hai naa? Everything alright?'

'Dad, I had got sucked into my ambitious world. I didn't realize that the one I was ignoring in pursuit of my dreams meant so much!' Vyom's eyes well up.

'...and that everything would seem meaningless without her... right?' his Dad smiles completing the sentence.

'Dad it is an unendurable stress to my mind, to my heart and... you are s.m.i.l.i.n.g.?'

'Do you know why? Because she still loves you.' Dad ruffles Vyom's hair affectionately.

'Who she? Do you know who she is?' Vyom looks like a child of three or four with his hair all tousled. When a child, he'd often approach his dad in the same manner and complain about some bully in the neighbourhood. His dad would say- '*pahle apne baal theek karo, phir batao kya hua...*'

'Pappa do you know who she is? Tell me no?' Vyom repeats.

'*Pahle apne baal theek karo...*' his dad laughs.

'*Pappa aap kuch bhi nahin bhule!*' Vyom beams.

'How can I?'

'*Aapne bigade hein, toh aap hi theek karo.*' Vyom bends smiling through tears.

'I know who she is.' His dad's clean shaven face shines with a stolen joy when he runs his fingers through his son's hair.

'Well...she is Tia. She loves me. Once she did...' Vyom settles his gaze on his dad's face, burning with the need to be nestled in his arms.

'Exorcise your ghosts once and for all. She still loves you boy! Know what? She got friendly with us, would daily come home on some excuse or the other, even cook for us at times and take care of your Mum the way you did...'

'Dad! AND you never told me! We were supposed to be good friends no?' Vyom can't give surety if he's awake.

'She wanted us not to.' Smiles the elderly gentleman warmly.

'All digested but for the fact that s.h.e. a.c.t.u.a.l.l.y. c.o.o.k.e.d.!!!'

'Believe me she did! Your *Maa* has trained her.'

'What about her result at Kota classes?'

'She was outstanding you know!'

'I don't believe all this! It's my third day here. Why have you guys been keeping secrets?'

172

'You didn't ask! We didn't tell! Simple!' Vyom's mother shoots a mischievous smile.

'*Maa!*' Vyom's lips curve into a full mighty grin, a strange lovely sensation tickling him through and through.

'That's nice *haan! Pata hai maa?* When she said she loved me, I was like *mere pass in sab cheezon ke liye time nahin hai* and I know I broke her heart. I did have a soft corner for her but...love? Well, now I feel trapped, you know. When she said on phone that she loved someone else...I felt...I felt I had missed the very mission of my life and was wandering around the house like...like I was completely lost *you know...*'

'We know.' His parents exclaim together as if by prior agreement. They're really-really happy.

'It's her *takiya kalaam*, not mine guys.' Vyom joins them.

'We know.'

'Haha! I know.'

'You know what?' asks his dad.

'Heehee. What?'

'Her parents are visiting us tonight.'

'Realllly? Well, I DON'T KNOW THAT!' he laughs.

The house sounds so alive!

'Hmmm. I hope you'll bring some refreshments on the way back home.' Says his Mom.

'Am I going somewhere?' smiles Vyom with made up innocence.

'You're going to see her.'

'Am I? Really?' Vyom stammered to a stop.

'C'mon! C'mon! Get ready.'

'Love you guys.'

Were those tears on his lashes?

...

*****

37

Nobodysround! A Kiss?

Vyom has reached at Tia's.

…

She is wearing an off-the-shoulder-top with a floral skirt. She has a more chiselled face presently with glowing peaches and cream complexion. Her high forehead speaks of her self-esteem. Her hair is perhaps longer than earlier, he recalls. Presently it is a long, wavy and golden brown bunch of hair falling brilliantly over her chest.

Her dazzling chocolate brown eyes bubble up on seeing him home.

Vyom is magnetized as if!

Both stand transfixed in the door way until Tia's mother shows up.

'Namastey auntiji.'

'Namastey. Namastey. God bless you.' she pats him as he bends to touch her feet.

'Hi!'

'Hiee!'

'So, how're you?'

'M fine. How about you?'

Both have a lot on their minds.

Vyom's heart longs to wrap his arms around her and cry uncontrollably.

What's the matter with him?

He used to be so strong!

Aah! That as when he hadn't fallen in love.

The fear of losing her has weakened him perhaps.

'Your favourite *adarak vali chai*.' Tia's mom breaks the charm hanging invisible somewhere between the two.

'Aap ko yaad tha?' he asks looking away shyly.

'You haven't been forgotten a single day in this house.' Tia seems to be controlling her emotions that however surface in her eyes again and again.

'Heard you've done outstandingly well son?'

'All your blessings and *someone's* good warm wishes may be.' answers Vyom with a naughty smile.

'Looks like *'someone'* wants a little more private time with you.' her mommy throws even naughtier a smile and moves out of the drawing room.

'Let me know Tia if anything needed.'

'Nothing needed mom. Please!'

'K honey!'

The awkward silence.

Both walking back through time may be.

Tia's kissable cherry lips open to say something but demur.

'So?'

'So?'

'Kahan se shuru karen?'

Tia apparently seems to be trying to keep her voice from cracking with emotions.

Her eyes glisten with moisture.

Was Vyom really there?

Or she had conjured him up with her imagination?

'So, that was a joke?' asks Vyom.

'A joke it could be...for I'd rather die a spinster than be somebody else's. I'd often chide myself for regressing into that fairy land of hope...which...which always suggested you were to be mine only.' Tia swipes her eyes with the back of her hands.

'Itna pyaar karti ho?' he fixes his gaze on hers.

'I love you.' Tia stumbles forward into his arms not able to contain any longer.

'Shhhhh! Your Mom may be around.' cautions Vyom though tantalized by a flash of her passionate glance.

'I don't care.' she blushes, every nerve of her body, vibrating.

'Chee! Aisa nahin kahte. Okay tell me...what do you care for?' Vyom holds her chin tenderly to ask.

'All I care for is to know whether you love me or not.'

'Well...I do..umm...kind of...you know...' Vyom laughs, trying to ease out of her embrace.

'What's wrong with you?' she grasps his wrist with suddenness.

'What's wrong with *you*? I'm at *your* home! *Your Mother* is around!' Vyom leans idly against a bookcase.

'Where to meet then so that you could hug me tight and say you loved me too?'

'Shhhhh!...okay...then...if that's what you yearn for. Right here! Right now! Now l.i.s.t.e.n...I. l.o.v.e. y.o.u. t.o.o.' whispers Vyom in a smouldering-spine- loosening tone.

He strokes her face adoringly, gives her a momentarily tight squeeze and then moves away. This is quite enough to send a wave of remembered fire up her body.

'Why move away?' Tia looks parched. She would like to scoot closer until she could lay her head against the sleeve of his starched white shirt.

Her eyes feast on his lips like a starved animal as if his lips presented a banquet of delicacies for her to devour all.

'B.e.c.a.u.s.e. my dear the only way to stop myself from loving you is...to move away.' he wonders from where he's got the guts to speak all that lay locked in his heart for years.

Tia moves closer again, gives him an ironic arch of her brows.

The intimate moments loaded with the zing and passion trigger something deep in is blood.

He throws a glance around.

'*Nobdysround.*' Tia whispers closing the distance before he could move away.

Vyom pulls her at once close to his lips and pecks from them, the tiny hammer of fear beating beneath his skin though.

His hands on her shoulders send zapping wires of electric desire through her.

Are they dreaming...?

One dream together...?

Well, yes!

*****

38

A Wrinkle in Love

Plus sized models, niche models, body part models and models with unique skills are some examples of specialty models. The base line parameters the modelling agents look for are - models need to have a specific body type, be within a certain height range and have good bone structure. First and foremost models need to be tall and slim; for the most part they need to be slimmer than the average girl. If you luckily possess these core ingredients, you have a good shot at making it as a model.

Have the right skills and personality and you jus' may be the next supermodel.

Sounds easy right?

Wrong!

This is the reason that the modelling industry gets such a bad reputation because the call for slim models could be seen as promoting an unrealistic body image. While this is a valid criticism there are some equally valid reasons that models need to be slender. Clothes hang better on a slimmer body and the fashion industry is essentially about selling clothes and other trappings of style like cosmetics, skin care, accessories, and perfumes.

The fashion industry's love-affair with skinny girls is not part of a conspiracy against average sized bodies. Slimmer figures are not only important on the runway but they also photograph better.

Other than the physical attributes what else makes for a good model?

The final thing agents look for is posture. Good posture is a modelling must as 70% of a model's career is runway modelling.

Unless you make it as a super-model, or build a glamorous catalogue career, making it as a model will mean walking a runway. Good posture and a solid walk are essential modelling skills but they can be learned. If a girl fits the mould in every way but lacks good posture an agent may still sign her with the hope that she can learn to stand straight and walk tall. However, if a slouchy model doesn't ever develop good posture she may find her career cut short. For this reason having good posture from the get go is a definite bonus.

As with any other job, personality is important as well. An ideal model will have a strong sense of self with well-developed self-esteem and a resilient psychological make-up. Modelling is stressful work and models are exposed to all sorts of potentially self-destructive influences. Modelling is a glamorous life and with the glamour comes an element of risk. Models are at a very great risk for falling prey to the trappings of glamour; alcohol, drugs, late night partying and unhealthy dieting regimes are always around. It takes a girl of strong character to face these things without succumbing to these temptations.

...

Our Aliya seems to have caught the eye of a modelling agent and he's desperate to sign her to their agency.

Aliya is but obvious elated.

She fails to realise he is an unscrupulous agent who loves to take advantage of eager young girls like her with a dream.

'What's wrong with you babe? A truly interested agent will never ask you for money.' Rohan doesn't seem convinced.

'What's the harm anyways? I think there's nothing wrong in paying for what you want.' Aliya argues.

'See, if an agent sees real potential in you, he knows, that is where they will make their money. They will invest in you and make their money back when they get you working. They will arrange for your test shots and only expect you to show up at the shoot on time and with a positive attitude.'

'Even they need money no? Are they supposed to pay for the photographers and the make-up artists? I'm still *nobody from nowhere*. I must not forget that no Rohan?'

'Aliya! You aren't getting it. Most agencies have agreements with photographers and make-up artists whom they pay to take their test shots and even build a working portfolio for an up-and-coming model. Models do need portfolios but when an agency is really interested in a girl and thinks she can make it as a model they will not ask for any money to help build it.'

'It's their business right? Why would they risk money on a newcomer?'

'Modelling is a business I agree. And businesses mean taking risks, a legitimate agency that thinks you can work as a model will take a risk on you.'

'What I'm worried about is not that I'll have to pay. I can compromise on that part. It's...' Aliya looks distressed. There's something she wants to share but she doesn't seem to be able to get through the waterfall of words.

'What's wrong? Is there something else he's asked you to do? Tell me no?' Rohan finds things fishy.

'He's asked me for a few nude or suggestive photographs.' Aliya lays facts bare, her knees tingling.

'Scoundrel! On what basis? How dare he?'

'Errr...he says he needs 'tasteful presentation.'

'Tasteful presentation my foot! When they ask you to take a picture in a bikini or even lingerie, they surely don't want you to look soft or somewhat innocent but overly provocative. If in the very first meeting they ask you to take a too sexy picture of yours for them, right away walk out the door and don't look back. That's what I know. And I don't want this crazy talk anymore. Is that clear babe?'

'I know this isn't common honey. But it is also not unheard of. It is a more common practice in small market agencies than in large market agencies. Small market agencies are usually local without an affiliation with a major agency and the work they get for you is on certain conditions.' Aliya explains.

'I don't care!'

'I think there's a price for everything.'

'You look ready to ...' Rohan adds untrustworthily.

'Perhaps I should be. The little money I'm left with has to go in the right direction or the entire sum will be squandered away in our meals.'

'Are you trying to tell me that you have been spending on me?'

'Am I wrong if I'm?'

'This would be coming one day. I knew it.'

'So, what did you plan to avoid a situation like this?'

'What do you expect me to do?'

'I expect nothing.'

'Listen babe!' it looks like Rohan is going to get one of his many bouts of panic right now.

'Please leave me alone for God's sake!' her face pales and then flushes back in a moment.

'I'm there with you!' he can feel frustration building inside him.

'That's the trouble! Now go!' she backfires.

Love, need, ambition, bitterness are as if pushing and shoving amongst themselves.

Rohan's worst nightmare has come true.

He's broken out in a cold sweat and is breathing unevenly.

He has to face it.

*****

39

Loneliness Sucks

Dear Diary

No time for greetings. I'm full. Need to urgently share what I've been through. You know I have been in Kota preparing for AIPMT. It's rightly called the coaching factory.

I have however come across some disheartening facts lately.

Parents decide what their children have to do. Up to this day! They tell their sons and daughters that they have very high expectations from them; that they are spending all they have earned till date in making them doctors or engineers so that they can live a successful life ahead...

What for God's sake, is the definition of a successful life?

They tell them every night that their selection is a must; they remind them each day '*hum tumhare liye jee rahe hein.*'

This is a BIG psychological pressure.

In schools up till class twelfth they have been performing wonders but as they come to career making, they are like s.o. m.u.c.h. p.r.e.s.s.u.r.i.s.e.d! And if their performance goes down by ever so little a per cent, they are depressed, like, beyond repair. If they tell their parents, all hells break loose! If they don't- the same!

They used to sleep eight to ten hours when they were in school life. Now what they utmost are able to spare is a five or six hours' sleep span. Believe me. I dream of the day when there will be no pressure on my brain and I would like...sleep EASY FOR HOURS AT A STRETCH!

Most of the parents don't try to understand their children. They want them to run in this marathon and be the winners too, no matter what! The things have come to such a pass that when parents call their children, they don't ask about their health, their mental state but the paper in Chemistry, Physics or Maths in which they haven't performed better than the last.

People here carve out little coops in their houses to let out to students and make a fortune. Looks like humanity is sleeping here and the only thing that seems to be alive is the test score.

Motivational lectures are arranged. The esteemed speakers will tell you what are the essential know-hows to be successful. Be it a goal to lose some weight, run a race, getting rid of an addiction or become a doctor...the approach has to be a dedicated one.

You know what? There used to be lot of rules and regulations in school life so we'd be upset at times and we would look forward to being in college *jahan par ki life masti bhari hogi...*

Nothing like that.

School life was better.

Kota...

Everything we need is here.

Things that we don't need are also here.

In abundance.

Masti bhi hai par sifr unke liye jinka koi fixed target nahin hai.

For those like me, it is...it is like being on a training ground.

A tough training under professionals.

If you underperform in some test series, you are demoted to the lower batch.

This feels like a stigma.

It breaks your confidence.

Ur heart too.

There comes a stage when there are only weak students around u.

U then forget that u used to be a bright student in school.

All you remember is a life that demands too much.

Don't bother about me. I'm doing pretty well. I'm in constant touch with Mom and Dad. But for the regular talk session with them on phone, who can say? May be even I could go in depression.

Dad says when loneliness grips or homesickness I must talk my heart out to some good friends or them, or be home to talk face to face.

It's much better and safer an option than going for an addiction where there's no recovery possible.

Heard about Trisha. I'm deeply pained. ☹

Yours

Anushka

*****

40

Somewhere Over the Rainbow

Skies are Blue...

Trisha is home.

'Mom please! Don't be so formal! I'll have something when I feel like eating you know. I'm not supposed to be a guest in my own home, right?'

'Yeah right but then...you haven't taken a morsel of grain since morning. How can I have unless you do?' Ragini asks with concern.

'Oh C'mon! I'm not a kid! Can take care of myself, no?'

'Trisha. Try n understand darling. Your Mom hasn't slept for two nights!' says Akshay.

'Is that my fault too Dad?'

'We aren't here to find faults dearie. We just want you to have something and then sleep.' says her Dad.

'Please Dad. What I want is a little peace. Sort out things. On my own. I don't need anything.'

What Trisha actually wants however is to press her head against her mother's chest and tell her how her heart aches for motherly love; how with each moment she finds her hopes wilt further.

'Okay.' her Dad nudges wife and the two leave her alone.

Trisha feels their faces bending to kiss her good night.

Her eyes fill with blinding spots.

...

Trisha knew such difficult situations would be there once she was home.

She wouldn't be able to face her loving parents while she was sober. It would prick her conscience, she knew.

She feels her cravings for drugs sparked, her breaths quickening.

She suffers from intense cramping in the limbs.

The anxiety makes her muscles and bones ache.

A sigh of pain escapes her lips.

She feels overcome by nausea.

'O God! O God! O God! This drug urge will kill me.' she cautiously closes the door.

She is utterly desperate.

She is trying hard to open the zip of her bag that seems to have got jammed.

It's like a pack of starved rats in a barn of rice.

Oh finally! She is panting hard but she digs out the little pills from her bag.

These are designer pills, very little ones. She pops up two in her mouth one with the design of a smiley and the other a little heart pierced by the Cupid's bow. Gone are the days when she would be able to feel the momentary high by just one pill. She would be out of the world during those ecstatic moments. Later however as she was getting into it, she realized one was not just enough to have her transported to the other world...it became the only stimulant for her to escape the unpleasant present. Not a drug left that she hasn't tried by now- Crack Cocaine, Ecstasy, Marijuana, LSD, Alcohol etc. etc. and even pain killers.

Her heart smashes against her ribs.

She feels her life to be wretched.

To escape the pangs of guilt, she lulls the wakeful perception of her soul under the spell of drugs.

...

Presently she is fast asleep, no sense of her whereabouts.

Akshay enters the room quietly.

He finds her cuddled in a heap on a single seat sofa, her head lolling to one side.

She looks beautiful and innocent in the flowery length of cotton as a dress.

She looks like a child who has been sleep deprived for many-many days.

The soft wheezes of hers and the angelic smile settled on her lip margins at once remind him how when she was a girl of three or four, she would cuddle around him in bed and how when he moved a bit, she would start muttering in sleep-'*Plz Dadda, sleep with me. Don't go.*' Akshay then would croon her to sleep, off key as Ragini sang much better. If she still refused to sleep, he would walk her up and down for as long as she didn't.

Memories stand out strong and vivid...

'*Dadda, I won't go to school today.*'

'*Why wouldn't my angel go to school?*'

'*It's Teachers' day tomorrow. Mom promised to bring me a nice card but she didn't.*' tantrums thrown with finger effect and stamping of foot.

'*Awwww! Is that all?*' croons *Dadda*.

'*Ummm.*' sings the pampered doll.

'*I have an ideeeeea.*' sings Dadda.

'*Kyaaa hai?*' eyes widened with surprise.

'*Hum ma'am ke liye card khud banayenge.*'

'*Sach?*'

'*Mooch!*'

'*Let me bring my colour kit.*'

'No. No. First Daddy needs a kiss.'

Her little head fits perfectly under his chin.

'Muaaaaaah! Love you Dadda! Mom maine aapko maaf kar diya.'

'Thanks your Highness!' bows Ragini.

...

Akshay is as if frozen in time.

Snippets of moments...

Images melt, change, are superimposed, one on another.

An acute spasm twists his face.

A tear or two lurk, quiver with the lip movement and then fall off making way through his cheeks first and then hanging at the tip of his nose as he sits slightly bent towards Trisha's beautiful face.

A tear rests on Trisha's brows, Akshay sweetly unaware of it.

Trisha is alarmed by her Dad's presence.

She doesn't open her eyes.

She relishes the touch that is perhaps the world's best touch ever.

Daddy's touch.

She wants more of it.

She slips her hand under his arm and he holds it firm.

Her eyes go mist and dewy. Her eye lashes stick together with tears. Her cheeks tremble. It's a great sense of relief...like...like she hasn't experienced really for long.

Akshay can't hold any more.

He begins sobbing which startles Trisha beyond words and at once she springs up.

Akshay hides his tears, contains himself, and looks away.

'Daddy.'

'Unh?'

'You love me still?' her lips shudder.

'How can I stop loving you, my child? It is simply beyond me!' he makes an effort to be able to speak, wipes his eyes only to find them welled again instantly.

'But...but I'm not a good girl any more Dad!' Trisha's voice goes heavy. Her face looks like a crushed piece of velvet.

'Who says you are not? Who says?' he cups her cheeks in his hands.

'My heart says. I feel it.' Trisha lets out a heart piercing cry that tears her lungs almost ripping them apart.

Muffled sobs.

'Nothing really clicks...Mom is never satisfied with me or my conduct. I think I can't fulfil your dreams...I'm completely messed up...ruin is staring in my face...I can see that. You don't know what I have been up to...' her words waver in the air.

'I know everything. Let's forget all that. Begin afresh? Hmm?' Akshay looks visibly relaxed.

'I very much want to...' doesn't however look sure of herself.

'Is that a need bigger than the need to be loved by your Ma and Pa?'

Glum silence.

'I will try Dadda...' she is somehow apprehending it will come again sweeping in.

'Look at yourself. These things have sucked happiness out of you! Sucked life out of you! I want my old Trisha back. Will I... get...h.e.r. b.a.c.k.?' Akshay holds her chin to ask as she sits by his feet on the carpeted floor, her legs tucked under her.

'Can't really promise...but...' she has squeezed shut her eyes. She is crying so hard that her body shudders and her indrawn breath rasps her throat.

Sobs burst out of both, intermittent.

'We'll try together. Okay. Tell me who are you missing the most. We'll meet that friend tomorrow itself.'

'I never missed any of my friends during all this time. I miss my class teacher at times though.' Trisha giggles.

'Thisss laughter! I missed this! Well, are you talking about... 'The Road...?' Akshay laughs too.

'The Road Roller...' completes Ragini, entering the room and sitting by Trisha.

'Aapko pata hai ek baar kya hua...' Trisha feels so light that she goes on and on.

Both Akshay and Ragini listen to her enchanted as when she had learnt to say 'Papa' n 'Mamma' for the first time! They nod at every word of hers, their eyes wet with hope and joy.

...

...

'Hi Diary

You know what I have been going through. Pray for me. Please please please oh God! I don't want to betray these gentle souls again. I really- really- really wanna be a good girl. I mean it. Insecurity is the most vulnerable button of mine. Despite this killing nausea making my senses go swaying, I feel like not giving up. May be I can cheat it the way it often does...AAH! I can hear the soft whizzes of Mom n Dadda. Perhaps after so long a time... they are sleeping sound like blessed angels. I wish I don't create a new disgusting scene tomorrow. Help me oh God!'

Hours are ticking by.

Trisha is not in her bed.

She sits on the window sill oscillating madly between panic and pride.

She is proud.

Dad still loves her!

And Mom too!

Is she fever-dreaming like in childhood she would?

The day is about to crack open.

She finds something remarkably serene about her.

She wants to carve a niche for herself.

For she chooses life...

...not death.

Her stomach lurches.

Her throat is filled.

The rising sun somewhere at distance flashes an encouraging smile.

Trisha begins to sing the song that always makes her spine tingle...

'Somewhere over the rainbow, way up high

There's a land that I heard of, once in a lullaby...

And the dreams that you dare to dream, really do come true...

Somewhere over the rainbow, birds fly over the rainbow

Why then, oh, why can't I?'

...

Her eyes next fall on some papers. Her Dad seems to have procured them from the resource centre. Looks like they are some informative brochures. She goes through them very carefully.

She has made the decision to enter rehab.

She is packing her bags.

*****

41

The Best I Had Was You!

Parents Bereaved

Anushka is home for a week. She has written the pre examination for AIPMT and her result is awaited. Presently she's lazing around in the house. Her Mom is on leave as she wants to spend as much time with her daughter as possible. She's watching TV.

'Omg! Omg!' she exclaims all of a sudden.

'What happened Mom?' Anushka is shocked to see her Mom look like a wrung- up mop rag.

'This is some news about...' her Mom has her eyes glued to the screen, emotionless as paper.

Anushka's Dad who has been sorting out some important papers at his desk is at once drawn to the news too.

Neither of her parents utters a word.

They just gaze each other in sheer disbelief.

It's ABP news channel on.

Again some student in Kota is reported to have committed suicide.

Anushka has never talked to the guy but she does recognize her.

It's one of her seniors Amit preparing for Mains.

Anushka can't breathe.

Things begin to blur.

Amit's father is being interrogated for details. It's an elderly gentleman with tears of remorse in his eyes, answering...

'It wasn't in the weirdest dreams of mine that my only son would commit suicide...he was a brilliant student. I'm absolutely unaware how he changed in this brief period of two-n-half a year! We used to talk often though he couldn't come home whenever there was a break as he said there was lot of pressure. We didn't want him to miss anything. We'd go personally visit him whenever we missed him intense. It was all fine-tuned...dunno why...' hiccups.

'...I was on a business trip when my wife called me the night ago. She made sure that I wasn't alone...that there was someone with me...I grew suspicious and the first nightmarish thought that struck my mind was...the same! ...i grew alarmed still promised her that I was able to handle the news calmly...that she could tell.' sobs hard.

Resumes- *'...all she could speak was 'Amit...shot himself.' The ground slipped from under my feet. I couldn't breathe a breath... aah! Thaa day! I had an impulse to talk to him the previous night but then thinking it was too late and he might be tired, perhaps gone to sleep...I had resisted...wish I could! Perhaps...things might have taken a different turn then...not this for God's sake!'*

Amit's mother- *'How I miss him! I feel rotten. How am I going to miss him every moment of my life! I'm not a strong woman. No more I am. I'm a vessel of glass; most vulnerable...he used to be so close to me...how could he hide things? When I'd be working in the kitchen...he'd startle me by coming in on tiptoes...and hugging me from behind. I'd pretend annoyance. I want him back! God please!'*

'Would you like to tell us about the video he made jus' before he err...committed suicide?' the reporter asks with compunction in her eyes.

'Yes when I somehow had a hold on myself, I checked his laptop to find some clues as to why did he go for such a drastic step, I was shocked to see his wallpaper. WHY DO I HAVE TO LIVE? was all that it read.' the old man breaks into uncontrollable grief.

'He'd nestle by me when five. He was a tender hearted child. He would be scared to visit the doctor because he hated syringes and medicines. How could he shoot himself? So cruel of him to have left us wailing behind!' his mother laments.

'He even made a video on his mobile doing the thing! It says he felt so broken and lonely...it says, 'Dad please mujhe maaf kar dena. We could've a good future together. I could've stayed home but you had ambition to see me at the top. I couldn't reach the top Dad! When I shoot my head with this revolver, it would slice open and you wouldn't be able to see. Still...' You might find me strong enough to tell you all this but it's the responsibility of my two daughters that keeps me alive. What father would have the heart to live on a day more having shouldered the corpse of his only son?'

'I understand.' the reporter's voice goes wet with emotion.

A brief pause.

'Would you like to say something to our youth watching this?'

'All I have to say is that if the idea of suicide strikes your mind, don't please stay alone. Come immediately in physical contact with your friends, relatives or parents at best. Better talk to them face-to-face. There's life beyond exams! Find a hobby; develop a passion that can be devouring your loneliness. Life is beautiful. It is precious. Amit, you haven't killed yourself. You have killed your Mom, Your Dad, your sisters whom you loved so much! Come back Amit!'

Anushka can't take any more.

She jerks away with a start, sobbing hard.

So is her mother.

Her dad switches the television off, shooting them a cool, unreadable glance.

The three come close enough to form a circle of love.

'Hope you...' her Dad can't give words to his apprehensions.

'Papa please! I'm a strong girl. I need not pass any tests to win your love. Do I?'

'You are the best darling! Top or not top, we love you always.'

Anushka can't still give surety if she's awake.

She wishes she wasn't.

*****

42

Don't Shrink to Fit In!

C'mon Now, You Gotta Have Fun!

Sarah's been a free bird since she broke off with Rohan. She's been trying various part time jobs and earning more than enough to satisfy her needs as a traveller.

Her bag pack is ready 24*7.

She isn't alone at the quest.

It's a group of girls burning with the same desire to keep moving.

They don't dream to settle with husband and home which is the average dream of an average girl.

Presently Sarah can be seen in deep pink top with puffy sleeves that partly hide her tattoo. She is enjoying a leisurely halt at a *dhaba* with her friends.

They are heading to Banglore.

This *dhaba* is known for serving local cuisine and truck stops. It's a typical dhaba scene as a wooden plank is placed across the width of the cot to place the dishes.

The food served, is typically inexpensive and has a 'homemade' touch given.

A paradise for travellers.

No doubt *dhabas* like this no more serve as the mere stop-overs.

They actually serve as the destination at times.

'Wow! My mouth begins watering *yaar!* What lip-smacking dishes! I love this Stuffed Naan and Daal Fry. These people exactly know how to win your heart. I love everything here. *Bhaiya!* Feed our gurgling stomachs please! Hee hee.' Sarah runs her hand over her tummy. She immediately checks herself as a foreign couple basking in the sun and enjoying black tea notices her, smiling.

'You love evrythn Sarah. What you couldn't love however was the poor sentimental guy you told us about, right?' one of her Sikh friends Preet asks.

Preet has dyed her hair temporarily. There're subtle sun-kissed highlights that give her luminosity an added charm. She takes out the beautiful little bottle of perfume from her bag and sprays a little on her wrists and neck. That's the perfume she always wears. Her manicured hands glow in the sun with the burgundy nail paint applied.

'Hee hee. Rohan? *Khote da puttar!*' exclaims Sarah, laughing.

'*O ji mainu kya je?*' asks the waiter confused. He is presently seen fiddling with the radio, from which cacophonous sounds begin to spurt.

'*O ji nahin ji.nahin ji!*' Sonia, one of the girls explains laughing.

Sonia is a not so tall a girl and has plain features. She believes beauty is a mind-set. You don't need a wiki page to remind you that you rock. She hasn't got her ears pierced, loves however to wear earrings so she wears ones that clip on her earlobes. She also loves to use other accessories like rings, necklaces, sunglasses, anklets, bracelets etc.

'*Vaise problem kya thi yaar?* I mean if he was so mad about you?'

'He must be going on well without me too. You know what? These guys have no moral grounds. They fall in love, fall out of love as per convenience you know. They are away from home. Need some compensation kinda. Moreover it's the sense of freedom that they indulge in things for. Poor kiddos!'

'Yeah right! *Vaise jo maza ghummakad hone mein hai, vo housewife ya beloved hone mein kahan!*'

'Know what Preet? My shoes were meant for walking. An ambitious girl, who just wants to win, should rather chase her dream than try men who chase skirts.'

'When a woman is ambitious, she cuts against the grain of her gender. You can't be ambitious and feminine at the same time.' says Preet.

'So you have to give up one or the other, right?' asks Sarah.

'Right' says Agnus, a sweet and quirky girl with a big grin. She is just seventeen years old; let that sink for a while. Despite her age, her style is fashion-forward and tasteful. She's age appropriate but edgy, and manages to keep her style feminine with a little flair. She looks like a perfect blend of magical and mythical. Her age doesn't stop her from exploring her fashion sense. She's kinda a sweet puzzle, with her Indian features and her defiant piercings.

'Wrong!' Sarah retorts with little irritation.

'Kya hua? Khana accha nahin laga?'

'Teri baat acchi nahin lagi.'

'You have to redefine both. And invent yourself in the process.' enlightens Sarah.

'A man is defined through work but a woman is defined through her roles and relationships to others. She becomes a shifting dynamic of wife, lover, mother, daughter etc. etc.etc. The best indicator of a girl's future success is not her IQ or GPA. It is rather the choice of her future husband.' Agnus adds disdainfully.

'Ambition however is central to the self. It's the inner voice that tells you that you are strangling yourself while keeping others at a higher pedestal. Trying to please them every time. You need to pull away from the role of an angel that you so much love to play all the time.' says Sarah stuffing dessert in her mouth.

'Yeah right! The good girl, the nurturer to put your needs last. AND I don't think even this can last for long. I mean a man will still find fault with you no matter what.' Preet is offered one more *gulab-jamun* which she accepts with a little reluctance.

'Hey! I don't wanna be fat yaar!'

'So...is any one of us dreaming to get married...!'

'No one honey.'

'Why then all this show about weight loss and slim figure, girls? We aren't supposed to be dainty dishes to feed somebody's lust. We are what we are. We should be happy the way we look. The way we are.' Sarah looks for approbation.

'Get shifted a bit. I need some more space.' nudges Preet to Sonia.

'Yes! That's the attitude! We need some more space! AND we need to speak this out. C'mon girls! Don't just shrink to fit in! Take up as much space as you need.' All giggle.

'Let me have one more *kulcha* then. Hee hee. This tongue slurping white butter is an absolute delight! The taste and the feel ummm...f.a.n.t.a.s.t.i.c! Who cares for the boys that take a girl to be a book? They buy the book by an attractive cover absolutely unable to judge what's inside.'

'Lassi was heavenly no?'

'Hmm it was!'

'But for this cute car Agnus owns, we couldn't dream of such crazy tours!'

'Then don't thank me. Thank my Dad who bought me this cute little car for us to see the world.'

They get into the car; bundles of delightful giggles.

The music playing in the car beautifully blends with the free spirits, the feel of freedom, the open skies...

'You work and work for years and years

You're always on the go.

You never take the minute off, too busy making dough...
Enjoy yourself...
Enjoy yourself...
(It's Later Than You Think)

*****

43

Up Again

Rohan has been working in a travelling agency for past two years. He badly needed a job back then. Any kind of job dammit! In addition to the formal education which he'd luckily acquired before falling a prey to Ecstasy and other vicious addictions, travel agents must be competent in computer and internet skills...that he was. Listening skills was the next pre-requisite... that he had in a pretty good amount. Listening to his *loves* was all he had been doing all these years.

Customer relationships and interpersonal skills that he needed to work face-to- face as well as on phone with his clients, he acquired bit by bit.

He had to have his Aliya back.

He kept messaging Aliya for days and months; couldn't have the nerve to ask if she had finally agreed to provide the pictures the agency demanded.

Perhaps he had no right to.

One moment he'd be all sorry not to have come up to her expectations as her boyfriend; the other he'd curse himself even for being in this world.

He'd miss his parents but wouldn't talk to them when they called.

The poor gentle souls however didn't lose hope.

They came over to Anurag's place to see their son. Their only son.

Such a scene of family reunion! Despite his pretended aloofness Rohan couldn't help falling at their feet in deep remorse and self-reproach.

He nevertheless insisted to live with Anurag than going back home.

He promised a fresh start and he did mean it.

...

He's been booking flights, cruises, rental cars and hotels other than resort stays and events. He's been simplifying the process of trip making for his clients by providing consultation services and entire travel packages.

His own life however seems to have been complicated.

This is not what he had wanted to be.

This is not what his loving parents had dreamt for him.

Anyway...

Rohan can presently be seen in his cubicle. He has to work year-round but is especially busy during peak vacation times in summers and winters. He spends long hours on the telephone or in front of computer terminals, making travel arrangements for his clients. This is the off-season currently so he is busy researching destinations learning about the latest offerings of prime travel resorts and locations.

In order to perform the required research he loves to keep up with travel magazines, books, journals and inline publications.

Leafing through one such magazine, Rohan has chanced upon what!!!

Aliya's picture!

It's an exotic place that the picture presents. Aliya looks more toned and more of everything, radiating an appealing smile! Such fine fingers, sculpted legs and perfectly pouted lips- the prized possessions he once had.

He blinks his eyes to make sure if it isn't one of the fancies that he often weaves when after the day's work; he is left to retrospection.

He feverishly runs his fingers over her rose bedecked hair.

His fingers go shaky.

The pang of longing is sharp.

A sudden fear snatches at his heart.

What if...?

No! His Aliya can't stoop down her self-respect even to materialize her dream.

...

Distance makes hearts grow fonder.

...

Rohan has a call from some unknown number.

Why! This is Aliya's voice!

Yes!

'Hello, is this SOTC?'

'Yes madam! How may I help you?' his heart is pirouetting madly on its toes as if!

'Errr...may I know your name sir?' Aliya too is hit with the warm thrill of foreknowledge.

'Is that you Aliya?' his voice trembles, wet with emotions gone raw.

'Rohan!?'

'It's me.'

'Omg! How come you end up here?'

'Eh, LIFE...How 'bout ya?'

'As a part of my modelling career, I'm being sent overseas – to gain practical experience ofc. Missed you so much baby!'

Silence pulsates hard between the two.

'Say something..'

'Main jo bolunga tumhe jhooth hi lagega.'

'Jhooth hi bol de!'

'I love you!'

'So...so?'

'So?'

'So, where am I seeing you today?'

'Not today I'm afraid.'

'Why?'

'Gotta buy smthn important.'

'More important than me?'

'Yes!'

'And u said you missed me the most? Tell me no what's that you can't buy later?'

'A ring, my love. Can't let ya go again.'

'I'm impressed! Omg! I'm hvn goosebumps!'

*****

44

Dream Big! Be You!

Our Anushka, as expected from a girl of her calibre, has topped the AIPMT Pre. She stands at the podium telling her success story to her comrades, answering their queries.

'Congrats Anushka!' a number of students cheer her in unison.

'Thank you so much! Thanks for the applause friends.'

'How do you plan to celebrate your success?' asks a studious young girl with twinkles in eyes and dimples in cheeks.

'Well, my Mom and Dad must have planned something wonderful for me. And of course I'm gonna celebrate with my friends as well.'

'Were you errr...sure of cracking the coveted medical entrance exam Anushka? Or...an accident you know, kinda.' giggles a boy asking.

'To be open and above board, I really was sure of cracking this exam but... bagging AIR was a dream I thought I could hardly materialise. To be a topper in any prestigious exam, you need to put in nothing but the very best of yours and of course perseverance counts a lot. I'm so glad that my hard work has brought cheers to my Mom, Dad and teachers who have been my intellectual mentors till today.' Anushka's voice goes wet with emotions.

'Do you guys have any more questions?' Anushka goes overwhelmed.

'Is every student preparing for AIPMT, entitled to success?' the question comes from where, she can't judge.

'A difficult questions I must say!' demurs Anushka smiling.

'You've topped the entrance exam. Do difficult questions still scare you?' a girl from amongst the students raises her hand.

'Ha ha! Well, no. Success isn't accidental you know. It's...a strategy I'd like to say. Once you have set a goal for yourself, you should be more than ready to go to any extent to achieve it.' Anushka's eyes meet the girl's.

'What stratagem should we follow to be on the safe side vis-à-vis negative marking?'

'You must have the conceptual clarity and the vision to identify the right option.'

'AND how can we develop that?'

'Whatever study material your resources provide you, go through it very carefully. Avail your resources well. And...common sense takes you long way like...say...you read something somewhere jus' causally; don't be causal about it...try to retain that piece of information in the wardrobe of your mind. God knows...it may be useful somewhere...n you are able to recall...like...well yes...! I did read it somewhere!'

'The course is so vast! I mean what approach required actually?'

'Cover each section, I would say. Do a background check related to any topic you're studying. Try to understand your strengths and your weaknesses. None else can do it better than you! Your perspective has to be deeper you know. Your approach has to be specific. It has to be utterly yours! Formulate your own strategy. That's what is going to help you!' beams Anushka, waiting for the next question.

'Should we go by guess or umm...leave the questions that we aren't so sure about?'

'Good question! Why not go by elimination? Think about the logical end of questions given. Use common sense as I told earlier. First look for the questions you're sure about. Attempt those first. Try to make linkages. That would give you a better understanding.'

'How should we prepare for the Pre? Is it a must to study hard for Pre as well?'

'PLEASE don't make any strict demarcation between the two. *Pre ke liye bhi aapko utni hi mehnat karna chahiye jitni ki Mains ke liye.* Solve as many test papers as you can. Practice! Practice! Practice! Practice is a must! Revision for Pre is a must! Take lot of mock tests. Regular mock tests help you analyse the time taken to solve the papers and find out what could be the possible change in your paper-solving strategy to maximise accuracy while keeping the number of attempts high. They help you to re-craft your preparation. Optimise your score! Don't please bog yourself down by the fact that u'll attempt only...say sixty or seventy. Weigh your options wisely. At first do give enough time to each probability. Later, try to maintain a good speed. Maintain accuracy as well.' Anushka inhales a lungful of air.

'How to prepare notes? Are notes essential?' looks like their questions are never going to end.

'Notes or no notes, is YOUR call. Really! It's no use if you go on copying things from various books until you're bored to death and damn confounded. Don't please proliferate ur material by copying things from the book as it is. Consolidate ur material. Then it is going to help you know.'

'I got it!'

'Who do you give the credit for this brilliant piece of success? I mean what's the key factor behind this spectacular performance?'

'To my parents and teachers of course! Had they not shown me this path...' tears lurk at her eye lids. 'I'm sorry...' she wipes her eyes to resume with a formal clearing of throat... '...umm...the key factor behind my success is my hard work, and my dedication of course to the dream of becoming a doctor.'

'Any message for us?'

'Be a better version of yourself. Each day! Work hard! Dream BIG!'

*****

45

Taking Life One Day at a Time

Spoonful of Life

Both Ananya and Navya have graduated from the high school. Navya plans a career in the fashion world. Her Mom and Dad seeing her keen interest have got her enrolled in the school of Fashion, Art and Design in Shanghai. The Fashion School offers a variety of courses in the areas of design, styling and business in response to the needs of the candidates. ...

Ananya is currently pursuing Hotel Management Course from the esteemed Institute of Hotel Management, Mumbai (IHM).

She is also running a blog named *Spoonful of Life* in which she describes how once being at the verge of self-invited death, she now is back to life, *taking life one day at a time.*

In an unabashed manner she shares how her parents had blatantly told her that she couldn't come home unless she promised to begin life afresh. After months of agony on both sides, her parents decided she could.

But there were some ground rules to be followed...

'Mom bought drug testing kits on eBay, and said I had to agree to random tests. She told me I had to be helpful around the house and try to be a responsible elder sister. I did my best...since I'm back to life and it is so good a feel that now more than anything I would like to help people. I would like to do some youth work, may be through this blog of mine too. I would do smthn to do with drugs counselling...Dad is proud of me.'

Dad says with tears in his eyes, 'I'm proud of what you have achieved. It was so very difficult to pull back from where you had ended up. You had to be really-really very strong to do it.'

…

Ananya is an articulate, positive young girl.

She's got her life back.

She's brilliant with her sisters.

Her sisters read her blog very carefully.

They jus' adore their elder sister.

Her blog says, '*Climbing up a mountain. Pulling yourself higher and still higher. Out of the abyss of pain, self-pity and misery. Things are brighter here. Sunnier here. Grass growing and the birdies chirping. Behold! The sun emerging out of the clouds! Don't lose your grip! Overcome thy fears. Once you start to slip...d.o.w.n. you go...exposed to the world's laughter. Remember you aren't the only fighter...there are many like you...climbing up higher and still higher...fighting their own battles...in quest of their own soul...their own life...a spoonful of life...*'

*****

46

The Sky is Everywhere!

'Dear Diary

Guess what?

I am back to life!

Aah!

What a tremendous feel of freedom!

Absolute freedom!

I always thought getting rid of family's control was all that freedom meant. I was wrong. Terribly wrong you know. Freedom means power. Power to be able to live, set yourself free. I have been through much...

When addiction strikes, it does without a warning.

It's a disease in fact.

You can't just quit it as if by magic.

There's help needed.

A structural help as such.

Mom and Dad provided me that help.

They provided me the tools to recover and thrive.

I'm no longer powerless over alcohol and drugs.

It isn't like that I'm never likely to be hit by the craving again but now I know how to hit it back.

The people over there, the doctors you know, they taught me how to work upon myself. It was perfectly safe and tranquil over there. Nobody laughed at me or judged me. They told me that real healing needed REAL efforts and a REAL time. They didn't lecture you know. They listened. And listening was all that I needed.

You have been a sympathetic listener too. For years. I can't thank you enough!

...

We had face to face talks. The doctors supervised each one like me, personally. They made us comfortable you know. They assured that my body wouldn't be thwarted by the process of detoxification. They called it the healing path recovery that led to an understanding between the doctor and the patient, you may say. The understanding led to empathy, empathy led to healing and healing eventually led to a more empowered life.

I was under residential program you know.

Mom and Dad came to see me often.

For them I had to.

I would feel paralysed earlier, trapped kind of, in this vicious circle of drugs you know. There was so much darkness in me that no light could shine on it! Detoxification was very hard you know but I knew that would help me become my true self again. There were moments of drowse, of cravings. I felt at times suicidal, insecure and miserable.

Every new drug was kinda new adventure for me earlier. I had decided to try anything that came to me. No purpose. Just fun. I had lost ten pounds in just two months! Still I couldn't just help. I wanted UP KINDA HIGH you know. Having tried so many drugs I had finally known that Cocaine was my poison. I knew I was gonna hit the peaking point with it...

What actually happened was that...I was at a friend's. Party was on. I was by myself- throwing out in the washroom. Nobody cared for me. I was not actually myself. I was screaming, throwing things, punching the wall like a savage you know...u know what? The hardest part of any HIGH is the COME DOWN.

COME DOWN was the biggest reason for which I decided to quit. It is...it is so painful when you get HIGH~ your body~ everythn~ goes up~ and then~ your body has to go thru transition~ BAD COME DOWNS you know. You are bed ridden for hours, days may be~ unable to sleep, eat, get up, and even breathe. If you try to get up, you'd surely fall or faint. No energy to live, no one to talk to, you feel so lonely, so lonely that you go insane, you are traumatized. Yr body burns...

Fine, I have never been bright at academics.

But I have been a leader at sports and you know that.

I realized in the middle of all that mess that I could take my life to the place where drugs could never take me.

Dad told me, assured me that I could be successful!

Drugs had been too taxing on me.

But I thought I should try at least for those who loved me the most in the whole world!

Mom and Dad.

Whenever the cravings returned in the course of my treatment I would remember how about the COME DOWNS were and why I had decided to quit. The thought would give me strength at once.

All said and done- the most challenging task before me now, is how to find a way to take care of myself.

Still there are wells of sadness and of pains inside me.

The love of my family and my true friends will surely heal me completely one day. Somehow I know thisss.

I'm so very thankful to God that I was somehow able to get my stuff together.

Guess what?

I'm going to school again!

The same school! My school!

I'm going to be very- very involved in school activities now.

I will surely be made the in-charge of things.

This drive to keep myself clean will take me to newer heights now.

And I will be an amazing person I tell you.

*****

Also by Maya Khandelwal

About the Author

Maya Khandelwal, happily married to writing, is a published author of three books My Favourite Mistake Ever, Just Zindagi and A Beautiful Mistake. She's also co-authored I Am A Woman, a fervent tribute to Kamala Das. A regular contributor to various online magazines, her articles about women as Engine Of Social Change have widely been read and admired. She has also been picked as one of the most esteemed women writers of India by #IncredibleWomenWritersOfIndia2016. Also nominated for the Sanmati Literary Award for the Best Woman Author 2016.

A wanderer at heart and with poetry running in her blood, her words strike a chord in the hearts of her readers where they echo for long. World Union of Poets has conferred the honour of being the President of the Virtual Gallery of the State of Rajasthan upon her.

Living her fairy tale love in real life, she's a happy person, at peace with life. A happy wife, a proud mother of two, Maya is a fish without water when not writing.